"This **REMARKABLE AND SIMPLE-TO-UNDERSTAND GUIDE** will show you how to get light, air, and good views; how to cut your material costs up to 90%; how to build greenhouses into your home; how to construct built-in root cellars, wine cellars, and fallout shelters; how to use solar energy effectively; how to build into hillsides and solve drainage problems; *plus* how to handle zoning and building codes. **IF YOU'RE THINKING OF BUILDING YOUR OWN LIVABLE, PLEAS- ANT, LIGHT AND AIRY AND TUNED-INTO-NATURE HOME, THIS BOOK IS FOR YOU."**

—*The Mother Earth News*

"Mike Oehler's **FASCINATING** new book shows that the construction of an underground abode needn't be just a daydream. Oehler, who has built several such structures and lives in one himself, provides **A COMPREHENSIVE TEXT** with numerous detailed illustrations . . . **EASY TO READ AND UNDERSTAND."**

"As built according to Oehler's various general designs . . . there are endless possibilities for windows, skylights and cross-ventilation. Mike shows how to go about the entire job step-by-step . . .

"**ALMOST EVERY QUESTION EXCEPT HOW TO ADD A BOWLING ALLEY IS ANTICIPATED AND ANSWERED THOROUGHLY . . . EXCELLENT"**

—*The Prairie Sun*

"Can you imagine this? Building a comfortable family home for $50 to $500 in less than half the time it normally takes to build. A house with 42 view-fed windows. Soundproof. Fireproof. Warm in winter. Cool in summer. Weatherproof. Ecolog- ically sound. Almost invisible. . . . a workable, livable and attractively organic house. . .

"The book is **FILLED WITH PRACTICAL DO'S AND DON'TS,** good illus- trations, some humorous side thoughts and lots of photographs.

"**IT'S A MUST FOR ANYONE WHO HAS EVER WANTED TO GO UNDER- GROUND."**

—*Northwest Exchange*

"Not at all conventional . . . uncommon taste . . . doesn't hedge . . . offers his seven years of experience in earth shelter building . . . **INTRIGUING."**

—*Earth Shelter Digest & Energy Report*

"A comprehensive how-to guide for the do-it-yourselfer. Oehler flatly doesn't like concrete, and the structural core of his sub-surface dwellings is what he calls the "PSP system" (post-shoring-polyethylene) . . . it sounds like **THE VERY BEST LOW-COST . . . HOME GOING.** Even if you're holding out for a guide on *concrete* underground construction, Oehler's book provides many times its cost in perceptive tips on sub-surface design, philosophy, living, and underground building in general."

—*The Next Whole Earth Catalog*

"If you want **A TRULY UNCONVENTIONAL HOME**, Mike Oehler has a book for you.

"Oehler has sold [50,000] copies of a book called 'The $50 & Up Underground House Book.' Now in its [fourth] printing. . . .

"It helps if you live in an area where there are no building codes, as Oehler does, but he insists that by using more expensive materials, anyone can build himself an acceptable home that can pass all building inspections."

—Spokane Spokesman Review

"Shares his wisdom and experience . . . Oehler and friends have developed homes — 'hobbit houses,' as he calls them — that are light, well ventilated, multileveled, and highly energy-efficient. The architectural possibilities are numerous; such homes can accommodate one person living simply or a large family. . . . profusely illustrated . . . authored by a seasoned homesteader . . . Oehler's years of experience and **SIMPLE, BUT FULL EXPLANATIONS** make this inexpensive mode of home construction **BOTH COMPREHENSIBLE AND TANTALIZING.**"

—NewAge

"**EXCITING ARCHITECTURAL CONCEPTS** . . . has developed his radical approach to underground construction through years of trial and error and practical testing while erecting two houses of his own, two more houses still a-building, and serving as a consultant on a number of other underground houses . . .

"His second endeavor, Mike's present home . . . contains some 375 square feet of living space and cost $500. . . . The book contains plans for much larger houses, modern in every respect."

—Barter Times

". . . fun to read because the author does not make this just another dry how-to what-not-to-do book but rather has a way of interjecting his own personality into it so you feel as if you are sitting around a warm fire talking personally with him. Full of pictures, plans, illustrations and ideas, this radical approach to underground construction **OFFERS MUCH FOR ANYONE CONTEMPLATING EARTH-SHELTERING FOR HIS HOME.**"

—Earthtone

". . . he has written **A WONDERFULLY UNSOPHISTICATED MANUAL** and filled it with design ideas and even plans for building in different ways and on different kinds of terrain . . . **IMPRESSIVE** . . . entertaining, sometimes philosophical . . . **A VALUABLE DOCUMENT.**"

—Daniel Lusk, National Public Radio

The $50 and Up
Underground House Book

By Mike Oehler

Illustrations by Chris Royer

The Great Chief in Washington sends word that he wishes to buy our land.

MOLE PUBLISHING COMPANY

The Great
Chief also
sends us
words of
friendship
and good
will.
This is kind
of him,
since we
know he has
little need
of our
friendship
in return.

Library of Congress Catalog Card Number 81-70112
ISBN 978-0-442-27311-8

Printed in the United Stated of America

17 19 20 18 16

Published by Mole Publishing Company

Readers are invited to use the design or construction methods and features described in this book. For permission to build from any specific plans write:

Mike Oehler
333 Gandhi Way
Bonners Ferry, Idaho 83805

Please include a self-addressed, stamped envelope with all correspondence.

 Printed on Recycled Paper

TABLE OF CONTENTS

But we will consider your offer, for we know if we do not so, the white man may come with guns and take our land.

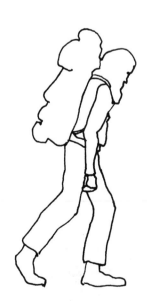

What Chief Seathl says, the Great Chief in Washington can count on as truly as our white brothers can count on the return of the seasons

INTRODUCTION

This is a highly personal book, perhaps too much so. I can't help it. I could no more write a dry technical manual than I could dance the Swan Lake Ballet. I have strong opinions, likes and dislikes. They are bound to find their way into these pages. If at times this book sounds like the drunk bellowing at the end of the bar, it was written, after all, by the drunk who is often seen at the end of the bar, bellowing.

My dislikes may offend you. Tisk tisk. So that you may brace yourself, or so that we may start off on the wrong foot—which ever —I'll list a few here. I dislike businessmen, the American medical profession, "liberated" women, most architecture, agri-business, 90 percent of industry, cities, pavement, the American philosophy of self-indulgence, strip-mining, clear-cutting, nuclear reactors, and anything having to do with recombinant DNA research and development. I consider television and the automobile two of the nation's greatest curses; the former because it rots the mind, the latter because it rots the body and destroys the land.

My likes may be equally offensive. I like the protesters of the sixties, beatnicks, hippies, yippies, back-to-the-landers (including the women who will sometimes these days offer you a cup of herb tea and serve it to you without a snarl), environmentalists, organic foods, the woods, wildlife, people who walk or ride bicycles, home-shop builders and back-yard tinkerers, fresh air, hard work, pure water, American Indians, saunas, my neighbors, my 40 acres, my dog, Bummer, and Nelly, my horse.

If you find the majority of these likes and dislikes offensive this is not the book for you. You won't really want to design and build a home which is integrated with nature. What you want is a concrete bomb shelter buried so that you may save your own fat ass during atomic attack. You don't want a home which is a growing, living thing, which has light and air and views (which is what this book is all about). These are not your values. You couldn't build a house yourself, anyway. The first time you swung an axe you would probably chop your foot. Don't read this book. Television's your medium. Slug your wife, beat your children and sit down and write me a hate letter. That's a better employment of your time. At least that way you'll work out some of your frustration.

There.

Now, for those who have survived so far . . . welcome. What we are going to try to do here is teach you how to design and build the most livable, pleasant, light and airy, the most in-tune-with-nature home you have ever entered. I've built several myself. They cost $50 and $500 each, including wall to wall carpeting in the latter case. That was a cost of about $1.35 per square foot as compared to the national building average of over $30 per square foot. To teach you to do this is a large task. But it is by no means an impossible one.

We have a number of things going for us, you and I. For one, I am not a trained architect. Not trained in a university, that is. So I'm not going to throw a lot of pedantic terminology at you to convince you that I'm really a brilliant dude and you are a little . . . well, just a little bit dumber. Nothing of the sort. We begin as equals.

My words are like the stars- they do not set.

5

If I have the experience, you have the will. If "I" have "invented" some new architectural designs, you can apply them. If it has taken me seven years of trial-and-error to get to my present degree of expertise, it could conceivably take you just seven days to assimilate most of it. If I had to start off blind—with no examples or texts to guide me—you have this book. That gives you a seven year running jump, a seven year advantage over where I was when I started. That's a hell of an advantage. That's a lot to have going for us.

We have more. If I'm not university trained (neither was Frank Lloyd Wright, if I may), this is only to the good. What they are teaching as the standard architecture curriculum in universities today is terrible. It's all concrete and glass. It's worse; it's a form of construction which is devastating to the environment. Modern buildings destroy wildlife habitat, take up farm land, waste energy, foul the air, help create adverse weather conditions, misuse material and are absurdly expensive. They are even gross eyesores once you learn to see it. Yet this is what students are *taught* to design. It's a long difficult process for an architect to overcome the brainwashing he's received in the course of his pursuit of that piece of parchment.

I didn't have to overcome this academic handicap. It was possible for me to start fresh, to look at architecture in a new way. Assuming that you have not had five years of brainwashing you will have this same advantage. Though the practice of truly good architecture is one of the arts, as much so as painting, it is possible for you to learn to design at least with competence. Under no circumstances are you going to do worse than what is being done by the vast majority of practicing architects today. Just by going underground you will surpass them. By using the methods of design explained later you will beat them hands down. Their houses won't even be in the same league as your owner-designed-and-built home.

Though not academically trained, I have lectured on underground architecture at more than thirty colleges and universities. At some schools, such as the Universities of Idaho, Washington, Oregon and New Mexico, I was sponsored by architecture departments, or by individual architecture professors. Not that the colleges today are open to innovation. Far from it. More schools refused than accepted the talks. Often I wasn't paid, the schools not considering it important enough a topic. Some places where I was refused flatly by the architecture departments the students themselves rallied, as they did at Berkeley and Harvard. They put me up, fed me, gathered an audience and even asked me to stay on.

This is not to bemoan my difficulties on campus. Rather, the significance of the years of lecturing was twofold. First, it gave me a proving ground for the theoretical aspect of my designs. Though there was occasional skepticism at the beginning of certain talks, and though I drew a fair number of professors, not *once* were the designs successfully challenged. The audiences invariably became thoughtful and bemused. New avenues had opened.

Secondly, the lectures forced me to present the material in a form which could be understood. By fielding questions then, I can anticipate your questions now. This is another of the things we have in our favor.

Few professional architects are going to like this book. That's fair enough; I like few professional architects.

They won't like it because to do so they would have to change their thinking. The professionals personify the status quo.

They won't like it because it teaches a do-it-yourself system which threatens their lush commissions.

They won't like it because it challenges their works. No one wants to admit that what he has been doing all of his professional life is wrong.

A few underground architects may be annoyed by this book. We use different materials and design techniques, they and I. But I think well of them. As long as they are going underground and are trying they deserve respect. There is room for differences of opinion and methods. Many of them have "hampered" their careers by stubbornly insisting on underground architecture. Commissions are scarce. Families must be fed. But a handful of resolute men have stuck with it.

Fortunately, they are about to be rewarded richly for their tenacity; underground architecture is soon to become very popular. Best guess is that within ten to twenty years it will become the most common form of construction in America. What's holding it up now is lack of public acceptance because of the preconceived notion of underground buildings as windowless, airless, basement-like buildings. When there are sufficient examples of fine underground architecture this notion will change. Acceptance by the public is perhaps only two years behind acceptance of solar energy, and insiders in that field expect a billion dollar a year business by 1981.

I am puzzled as to why the professional underground architects have not yet stumbled onto the Uphill Patio concept, the Offset Room and the Royer Foyer. With the exception of my own house and a handful of recent owner-designed-and-built underground structures in Northern Idaho I know of no other buildings employing these techniques. I don't even know of a single case where the pros have used the clerestory concept—a natural for underground buildings—though it is a common architectural technique, listed in every text on design.

If the professional architects, both above and underground, have one common failing, it is their reliance upon new, industrial produced building materials. Who among them is insisting upon salvaged windows? Who among them encourages builders to work up material native to the site? Even in forested areas, what architect has seen the wisdom and economy of using whole timber construction—logs—which have been felled, seasoned, peeled, treated, stained and varnished by the owners or builders themselves, eliminating the high cost of logging, milling, transporting, advertising and marketing with the corresponding markups at each step until, in the end, the cost is outrageous?

I am not certain why the architects share this failing. Some perhaps are frightened that locally produced materials might not meet specifications. Others undoubtedly insist upon the higher priced materials because their commissions will be higher. The heart of the problem may lie in the fact that most architects are city raised and educated and simply have no idea of the possibilities of locally worked materials. Of them all, only

the underground architects have taken a step in the right direction; they at least are using earth native to the site. This, the finest of all building materials, is dirt cheap.

I will ask one thing of you. When you begin your project please, *please* stick to the five approved principles of design. I can't urge you too strongly on this point. It is vital to the success of your structure, especially if you go the PSP system, which I urge on you just as strongly. The five principles combined with the PSP system and the earth/carpet floor are the nucleus of this book. Together they will give you a house which has light, air, views and charm; an aesthetic delight. Together they can save you up to 90 percent of your building costs.

You may be tempted to experiment from the beginning, to try something "new." Chances are what you think is new is not new at all but something which we have rejected for theoretical reasons, or because we have tried it and it has failed, or because we have seen it fail on other structures. Build with the methods which are proven successful and you will have a successful house. Then when you add on later you may experiment, and if the experiment fails, you still have that livable home to fall back upon.

* * *

At the risk of losing my credibility with you; at the risk of having you think me a plain raving NUT, I'm going to throw out one final offering here. It is a discovery I happened across five or six years ago. It is a means of asking for and receiving instant advice from a source more knowledgeable than is to be found on any campus or library in the nation. It can help you on the design and building of your house, and in many other ways. It is a method of plugging into an information network much more sophisticated than all of the electronic/satellite/computerized systems combined. It's yours for the using, and it's free.

I call it consulting the Great Potato. I happened across this discovery after several amazed years of consulting the *I Ching*, or *Book of Changes*. Are you familiar with the *I Ching*? It has been one of the two or three most influential books in Chinese history— a book on which all of the greatest Chinese

The idea is strange to us.

7

Yet we do not own the freshness of the air or the sparkle of the water. How can you buy them from us?

thinkers have been working for the past 4,000 years. Confucius, among others, worked on the *I Ching*. You don't merely read the book, you consult it for it is an oracle. It tells you what changes are coming ahead in your life, and how to deal correctly with these changes. If you have a problem it tells you how to deal with the problem. Since the 50's the *I Ching* has become the most influential book in American art circles, and among the young seeking alternatives. It has become this because it works.

The secret to the workings of both the *I Ching* and the Great Potato is chance. Chance? Yes. The ancient Chinese believed that the Divinity expressed Himself in three ways; through the creation of plants, animals and man. In order for there to be a fourth mode of expression which we could understand clearly when asking for help (praying) the Chinese utilized chance, because *chance of itself has absolutely no meaning*. Because it has no meaning, a deeper meaning can come into it. By utilizing chance you can receive a direct answer to a question asked of God.*

How do you utilize chance? By flipping a coin. In the case of consulting the *I Ching* you flip three coins at once and do it six times. This tells you where to look up the answer to your problem in the book. (The mechanics of this are too complicated to go into here. If you are not familiar with the *I Ching*, I suggest you find some young person who is— many long-haired back-to-the-landers, young adults, or college people could help you. The best translation to use is the Wilhelm/Baynes translation published by the Princeton University Press.)

In the case of consulting the Great Potato, you flip one coin one time. You state a question in your mind (or out loud to perhaps

skeptical friends—as I say, they may think you're finally gone around the bend), you do a little quick praying, and you flip the coin for the answer. The question should be one which has an unknown element in the future. It may be as simple as "Should I go to the store today?" or as complicated as, "Should I add another room to the house?" If you are receptive to the Forces Beyond, you will get the correct answer. To find out whether you are receptive, I'd suggest getting into the *I Ching* first. There the answers are printed out in black and white and it will soon become apparent whether the system will work in your case. It doesn't work for everyone. Not everyone is receptive.

More decisions about the design and construction of my house were made in this manner than I'd care to admit. In fact, I may do some subtle bragging in this book about "discovering" or "inventing" such features as the Barbecue Windows, the Uphill Patio, the Offset Room, the Royer Foyer, and others. The fact is, however, I was guided to these discoveries, sometimes while consulting the Great Potato, sometimes by other means. It was not due to any special ability or creativity on my part. The Forces Beyond led me to these discoveries. Just thought I'd give credit where credit is due.

---

*It is interesting to note that the most recent government of China, the Communists, have made repeated attempts to ban the *I Ching* and its use. This has caused considerable puzzlement and distress among young, American long-haired Mao worshippers. The reason for the attempted suppression is easy to understand, however, when one recalls that a central axiom of communist dogma is that there is no God. Any book and system which not only affirms but *proves* the existence of God is therefore a threat to the whole of communist theory. The suppression has never gotten very far. The book keeps popping back up.

Chapter 1
WHAT AN UNDERGROUND HOUSE IS NOT

Perhaps we should start with what an underground house is not. An underground house is not dark, damp and dirty. It is not airless and gloomy. It is absolutely *not* a basement.

An underground house
   has no more in common
      with a basement,
Than a penthouse apartment
   has in common
      with a hot, dark, dusty attic.

A basement is not designed for human habitat. It is a place to put the furnace and store junk. It is constructed to reach below the frost line so that the frost heaves don't crumple the fragile conventional structure above. It is a place where workmen can walk around checking for termites under the flooring, where they may work on pipes and wiring. Its design, function and often even the material from which it is built is different from an underground house. A basement is usually a dark, damp, dirty place and even when it is not, even when it is a recreation room, say, it is usually an airless place with few windows, artificially lighted and having an artificial feel.

An underground house is not this at all.
It's not a cave either.

We will decide in our time

9

Chapter 2
WHAT AN UNDERGROUND HOUSE IS;
23 ADVANTAGES

We believe that when designed and built properly on suitable sites, Post/Shoring/Polyethylene, or PSP, underground dwellings are the finest that can be constructed. They have 23 distinct advantages over conventional structures. These are:

1. NO FOUNDATION.
2. LESS BUILDING MATERIAL.
3. LESS LABOR.
4. MOST AESTHETICALLY PLEASING.
5. LESS TAX.
6. WARM IN WINTER.
7. COOL IN SUMMER.
8. BETTER VIEW.
9. BUILT-IN GREENHOUSE.
10. ECOLOGICALLY SOUND.
11. INCREASED YARD SPACE.
12. FALLOUT SHELTER.
13. CUTS ATMOSPHERIC RADIATION.
14. DEFENSIBLE.
15. CONCEALMENT.
16. CLOSER TO SOURCE OF WATER.
17. RELATIVELY FIREPROOF.
18. PIPES NEVER FREEZE.
19. SUPERIOR FLOORING.
20. CAN BE BUILT BY ANYONE.
21. WEATHERPROOF.
22. LESS MAINTENANCE.
23. SOUNDPROOF.

(1) On conventional houses, FOUNDATIONS are a considerable percent of the total cost of the house. We eliminate that cost right away. In fact, the cost of pouring a conventional foundation is often what it costs to build an entire underground house.

Foundations serve a number of purposes on surface structures. First of all, obviously, they support the building. Secondly, they reach below the frost line in cold areas to eliminate the threat of frost heaves damaging the structure. Thirdly, a foundation raises the house above the earth so that the flooring is not rotted by moisture. Lastly they make possible a crawl space (where there is no basement) so that the utilities and termites may be worked on without tearing up the floor.

All of this is unnecessary. The PSP method is to utilize pole construction and to sink it below the surface. Pole construction is as sturdy or even sturdier than conventional construction. Pole construction was invented in Japan to deal with earthquakes. With a conventional building you are in real trouble if an earthquake or other disaster crumbles your foundation; the house may likely come down. Pole construction does not crumble, however. Each pole rides out the quake, shifts around as it must, and settles back into place leaving the building comparatively undamaged.

Every part of this earth is sacred to my people.

(2) There is LESS BUILDING MATERIAL used in underground construction. The fact is with PSP we use about half the amount of material a conventional structure uses. Except for polyethylene, the only thing we use more of, probably are windows. See page 25 for a comparison of materials.

(3) With less material we use LESS LABOR simply because there is less material to handle. If the house is dug by hand this advantage is somewhat lessened, but it still may involve less labor. By way of example, a friend began construction of an A frame cabin about the same time I began work on the original $50 U house. Both buildings had about the same amount of floor space. Though his was on a site where the materials could be delivered by truck and my materials had to be back packed a quarter of a mile over a 200 foot hill, I finished mine in two months while it took him nearly nine to complete his. And my house was dug by hand. When a U house is dug by machine the labor is reduced to minimum levels.

(4) An underground house is the most AESTHETICALLY PLEASING of all the modes of construction. When completed a U house is nearly invisible. Rather than looking at a ticky tacky box of painted lumber and roofing or a hunk of concrete and steel you see only grass, shrubs and trees. An underground house blends in with the surroundings. It does not compete with or try to dominate the environment.

It comes down to this: which is the most pleasing, what God has created or what man has created? Would you rather look at hunks of concrete, or at aluminum siding, or would you rather look at the natural greenery? A U house blends in with nature while the other is constructed, usually, with a total disregard for the environment. Those few above ground structures which do merge with the surroundings are so unusual as to sometimes become world famous. Frank Lloyd Wright's Falling Water house in Pennsylvania is an example of one such. Yet, a good subsurface structure blends with nature even better than that.

(5) You pay LESS TAX on a U house because it has less resale value (at this time) than do other structures. As their popularity increases this blessing will be wiped out, but for now it is a happy advantage. When the assessor comes around to see your house—assuming he can find it—you can feign great surprise and indignation and wave the assessment in the air and point out that no one in their right mind would pay that much for *a hole in the ground!*

(6) Our houses are far EASIER TO HEAT in the winter than are conventional buildings. We call this the root cellar effect.

Since one of every twelve B.T.U.'s consumed on earth go to heat or cool an American structure, underground buildings, when they become more common, will have both national and global impact in terms of energy savings. For the individual home owner the root cellar effect means cash in the pocket.

If the average temperature of the earth surrounding an underground house is 50 degrees and the air temperature falls to zero, the man living below must raise his home temperature by only 22 degrees while the man living above ground must raise the home temperature by 72 degrees.

(7) The root cellar effect applies equally to the summer months making the U house far EASIER TO COOL. Not only does one have that 50 degrees of refrigeration to draw upon but there is the transpiration of the grass and other vegetation on the roof to add an additional cooling factor. Lots of windows opened at night can keep the air circulating pleasantly and keep the humidity factor—admittedly sometimes a problem in U houses —to a minimum.

(8) Underground houses can actually offer a BETTER VIEW than above ground dwellings. This is such a mind boggling concept, so alien to normal concepts, that we will go into this in detail in the chapter on design.

(9) BUILT-IN GREENHOUSES are a feature which is superbly applicable to U housing. Even the federal government has recognized the wisdom of attaching greenhouses to dwellings for both food production and solar heating—it has been making funding available for experimentation in this direction.

On all housing both above and below surface attached greenhouses not only provide a means of food production and solar heating, but when built around windows they help to keep heat escapage to a minimum, the same way storm windows do. When these greenhouses are built below the surface as with U

Every shining pine needle,

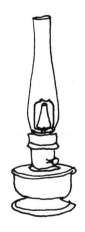

housing and as with the old-fashioned farmer's grow hole, they also have the benefit of drawing on geothermal energy.

(10) U housing is unquestionably the most ECOLOGICALLY SOUND form of building presently developed. The use of less building material means less disruption of the environment, especially since most of those materials are of a renewable source (lumber). The use of less energy to heat and cool these structures is, certainly, a big eco plus. And then there is the fact that U houses take up none of the earth's growing surface. About this, conservationist-architect Malcolm B. Wells says:

"We the people of the United States of America, and all other animals upon this continent, spend our lives in utter dependence upon living green plants. They alone give us our food. They alone renew and refresh the air. They alone heal man's earth wounds . . . They alone store sunlight for our use.

"But few of us realize all this.

"We forget that green plants must have ground space in order to live and grow, so we cover the life-giving land with buildings and roads at ever-faster rates, often in low-lying areas where the soil is richest. And that's not all. The buildings we're building today waste massive amounts of fuel and water, they intensify noise and weather, they're out of step with nature's grand century-by-century pace, and they're crushing the human spirit.

"We don't know the first thing about building.

"Therefore, those of us who pave and build are helping to plunge the nation into disaster. It's as simple as that—today's architects, engineers, builders, pavers, realtors, developers, planners, building officials and code administrators are public enemies— destroyers of life. There's no other way of looking at it in the light of today's knowledge. Our grandchildren are going to curse us for our blindness."

Just one small example of how we are destroying the environment for living green things: Between 1920 and 1950 one third of the farm land in Ohio was eroded away, strip mined, built upon or paved over. Obviously the destruction has continued apace. And that's just one of our fifty states. The result is seen in such effects as the 10 percent increase in carbon dioxide now measurable in the at-

mosphere. Building underground is a small way that an individual can help to counter this trend, but it is an important way. The environment will become healthy again only when each of the 220 million Americans work in small ways to promote that health. If we don't, of course, we will not survive.

(11) Another happy advantage is the INCREASED YARD SPACE one gains by building underground. The roof makes a dandy lawn. If the average house takes up a third to a half of any given plot and that plot costs, say, $10,000 then the home owner gains $3,500 to $5,000 worth of usable yard just because he has built below surface.

(12) The fact that a U house can also be a FALLOUT SHELTER is yet another advantage. A great number of people ranging from a group of prestigious Harvard professors, to those who study the Bible, to the entire Chinese population (who are burrowing like crazy beneath their cities), anticipate a global atomic war before the turn of the century. We won't go into that anymore here other than to point out that with three feet of earth on the roof and the proper design a U house can meet fallout shelter specifications.

(13) Similarly the effects of ATMOSPHERIC RADIATION, steadily increasing with each atomic test and nuclear plant constructed, can be lessened by living underground.

(14) DEFENSE is something few people think of when building a house. This past century, since the Indians have been squashed, there has been little need for defensive homes in the United States.

Yet an awareness of the need for defense has been increasing with the rise in the crime rate. Whole subdivisions are being built now with fortified walls around them and manned gates. One new subdivision in California even has a defensive moat around it. If, as many fear, this fragile industrial society of ours collapses, the need for a defensible home could be paramount. A person might not be sufficiently alarmed to design a structure with defense in mind but it might be reassuring to know that one's house is defensible should that need arise. All underground structures are defensible. Where does the army go when it wishes to defend itself? It goes underground.

(15) CONCEALMENT may in the end turn out to be the best defense from both the pillaging bands of people which would be the inevitable result of a collapse of this society, and from the harassment of building inspectors and other government criminals which is the inevitable result of a continuation of this society. If they can't find you they can't attack or harass you. And there just is no more concealable structure than one which is below surface. Entire armies were hidden underground in Viet Nam and the most sophisticated electronic gadgetry in the world failed to ferret them out. If so, a man could certainly hide his family underground. More on this in the section on building codes.

(16) You're CLOSER TO A SOURCE OF WATER in an underground house. This is an advantage which might not appeal to a person with lots of money, but to the homesteader who digs his own well, or who pays to have it dug, it is a happy advantage indeed. By sinking your well inside your perhaps 10 foot deep house, you have a 10 foot savings. If the well is professionally driven this means, in our section of the country, a savings of $200, or four times the cost of the original $50 house. If it is dug by hand, it means a savings of up to a week of grunting and groaning. If you sink a ten foot house and the water table is twenty feet down, you are half-way there. Of course, you will want to be pretty sure that the water table is down at some depth before beginning the house. If you sink a ten foot house where the water table is six feet deep, you will wind up with a four foot swimming pool.

(17) A U house is RELATIVELY FIREPROOF. Certainly the sod roof is never going to catch fire from stovepipe sparks as do the shaked or asphalted roofs of many conventional houses. An earthen floor is not going to burn. Even the walls, though built of wood, are fire resistant since they are solidly backed with earth. Air can reach only one surface. The walls of frame houses have at least four surfaces exposed to air. Furthermore, the material can burn in tandem; when the interior paneling catches fire it ignites the building paper which ignites the exterior sheeting. Each of these materials helps to raise the kindling temperature of the other material further up the line until soon you have a conflagration all but impossible to stop especially out in the country where fire protection is inadequate or nonexistent.

Heavy wooden beams are reported to do better in a hot fire than do steel girders. They tell the story of a fire in a structure near Chicago which was partially built with wooden beams in the old section and steel girders in the newer part. When a fire gutted the building the steel beams melted and collapsed. The wooden beams burned only about an inch deep. They formed a layer of charcoal on the outside which blocked the oxygen. They were still standing after the fire.

(18) Your PIPES WILL NEVER FREEZE in a Hobbit House. They are safely buried in warm earth beneath your floor. Above ground structures with crawl spaces are highly conducive to frozen plumbing as just about everyone who has ever lived in cold country has learned with sorrow. The wind and cold whistles into those crawl spaces and the pipes have to be wrapped with insulation or heating elements, the toilets adjusted so that they keep running slowly, and so forth. Even so, the pipes sometimes freeze anyway. Houses with full basements run less risk but are still not immune. Huckleberry Duckleberry Farm, a former North Idaho commune, lost water in the main house for four months in the winter of 1972. Pipes didn't thaw till April. This despite a full basement with a wood furnace.

(19) Which brings us to one of the least recognized benefits: SUPERIOR FLOORING. There is no finer flooring than a carpet on earth. The floor stays warm all winter. It doesn't rot, get termite infested, make noise when walked upon, or ignite like wooden flooring. When tromped upon day after day it doesn't cause varicose veins, fallen arches, leg cramps or any of the other ailments associated with constant walking on concrete floors. Your feet were *designed* to walk on earth. This is one of those things which is so obvious that few people can see it.

A layer of polyethylene between the carpet and earth will keep both the moisture and dirt from working up through the rug. If anything should go wrong with the pipes beneath the floor you don't have to call in a jackhammer man like the person with the concrete floor does, or crawl around on your back in a two foot high space like those with wooden floors and crawl spaces must. In-

every mist in the dark woods,

13

every clearing and humming insect, is holy in the memory and experience of my people.

stead, when there is a problem, or when you wish to add to the plumbing or run another electrical conduit, you simply roll back the carpet and polyethylene, grab your shovel and have at it.

(20) These houses are so simple they CAN BE BUILT BY ANYONE. The only place where there is any heavy effort is in working with the posts and beams. Someone can usually be found to help there, as they can with the windows and utilities. The rest of the job is simplicity itself. Nothing is easier to frame than a shed roof. The floor is little more complicated than leveling earth and rolling out carpet. Siding-off the building is as simple as stacking lumber and shoveling earth.

(21) A U house is as WEATHERPROOF as a structure with external windows can possibly be. Where do folks go in the midwest when a tornado approaches? They go underground into tornado shelters. Trailer houses and similar mistakes are usually totally destroyed when a tornado or hurricane hits. Even if a full sized tree should fall on a U house the survival chances are excellent for there are banks of solid earth on all sides to absorb the weight. If a tree falls on most conventional structures devastation is the result. It makes a man shudder to even think of what happens when a tree hits a trailer.

(22) There is LESS MAINTENANCE needed on a U house. As mentioned the floor is virtually maintenance free. So is the exterior. You should never need to re-roof the place, nor will you ever need to paint the outer walls. Exterior maintenance is so simple, in fact, that mowing your roof could be your biggest problem.

(23) The final great advantage is that a U house is relatively SOUNDPROOF. Obviously, no noise is going to sneak in through the floor or through those solid earth walls and darn little is likely to make it through eighteen inches of earthen roof. That leaves the windows and doors as sound conductors. Even here we have the advantage of having most windows facing out onto sunken courtyards which in themselves are sound sheltered areas and as little sound enters, little sound escapes: you are far less likely to disturb your neighbor even if you make outrageous noise.

14

Chapter 3
HISTORIES OF THE $50 AND $500 UNDERGROUND HOUSES

I built the original $50 underground house in the spring of 1971 with help from a friend, a man named Lynn Moore. From the beginning the house was different from any other both in design and materials.

A winter spent brooding over design had led me to reject what I've come to call the First-Thought House. This is an underground built into a hillside with windows rearing above surface to give a view down hill. For months it was the only design I could imagine though I was troubled by predictable drainage problems, by the fact that there could be entrances only on one side of the house, and because I couldn't figure out how to get cross ventilation and a balance of light.

In the end, we did a radical thing. We built so that the contour of the roof was the same as the pitch of the hill. This solved much of our drainage problem for all precipitation landing on the roof ran off away from the house. The windows, rather than facing down hill, faced up. At first these were to be basement type windows, but that didn't seem right. If we were to have windows there why not full sized ones? Then it seemed only logical to stack windows one on top of the other making nearly a solid wall of glass from waist-high to the eight foot ceiling. What could have been a gloomy back wall became light and airy.

There wasn't much of a view out there. We began excavating on the outside and put in an uphill sunken patio. We planted trees and landscaped it somewhat and it looked nice. We put in a door there, too, since the excavation was already completed outside.

One afternoon well before the house was completed I was sitting on the floor feeling mellow, laid-back, you might say. A cloud apparently cleared the sun for all of a sudden a shaft of sunlight came in through an uncompleted section of the west wall near the roof. My head snapped up like a retriever getting a scent. I knew instantly that I just had to have a window there to catch the evening sun. Shouting, "Yeah, yeah, oh yeah!" or something to that effect, I ran outside and grabbed a shovel. Twelve hours later I had a window in and shoring on the excavation outside. That was the firewindow.

We built the structural part of the house out of cedar and tamarack logs I'd felled a year before when my plans were for a log cabin. For paneling we used two-foot long millends—lumber that was slightly defective and trimmed off by the planer at the local saw mill. The mill threw these away. They were free for the taking. The idea to use polyethylene on the roof came from Hew Williams, founder of Tolstoy Farm over near Davenport, Washington. Hew had a six-sided log cabin with a three-foot sod roof which unfortunately leaked mud during rains. He shoveled off the roof, laid a layer of polyethylene down, four inches of dirt, another layer of polyethylene and the full complement of dirt and sod on top of that. I've never seen any reason to change his formula except to use less earth and pitch the roof. Hew was also the first to show me the benefits of an earth/carpet floor.

The idea to use polyethylene around the rest of the house came from Lynn Moore.

We know that the white man does not understand our ways.

15

One day he said, "Why don't we use it outside the walls? It'll keep the wood from rotting." And that was the beginning of the Post/Shoring/Polyethylene system.

Total cost of materials for the house was just under $50 including stove and a lamp. It would be higher by today's prices. When I bought my last air tight stove, for example, it was $35, not $22, without pipes and damper. If you can't scrounge free lumber, salvage it, or mill it from trees on your own land with a chain saw and an Alaskan Mill, the house could run in the hundreds. But if you can get the lumber, and if you can weld together your own stove from perhaps an old thirty-gallon oil drum, it is still possible to build a house like this for under $50. Here's the breakdown on the original one:

Beams & Posts	Free
Millends (lumber)	Free
Polyethylene	$15.00
Nails	$ .50
Flooring	Free
Insulation	Free
Paint	$ 2.00
Chairs	Free
Tables	$ 2.20
Door	Free
Cooler	Free
Lamp	$ 4.00
Stove, Stove Pipes & Damper	$22.00
Windows	$ 4.00
TOTAL	$49.70

The cooler and door were given to me by a neighbor who was tearing down an old cabin. The nails were bought at a local junk sale. They were used so I had to straighten them one at a time. The windows were also used. In those days before the rush of back-to-the-landers I was able to buy them for 25¢ and 50¢ each. The lamp was a kerosene model bought at a local hardware store. I needed a single quart of paint because I used it only around the windows, preferring to keep the beams and paneling natural. The chairs and tables were made out of logs and millends, the only cost there being oilcloth table covering, that turn of the century kitchen favorite which not only looks pretty, but which can be cleaned with a damp rag. The insulation was Mother Earth herself, some thousands of miles thick and absolutely free.

The flooring presented a problem which was solved by 14 year old Mary Ann, daughter of John and Mary Van Etten, close neighbors and friends. I was complaining about my dirt floor 'cause it raised dust and was no fun to sit on. I wasn't about to do a wooden floor for various reasons and she suggested I try straw. Since her father wanted to clear the old straw out of their barn for the new hay cutting, he gave me a number of bales for free. It made great flooring. It reflected light and made the place cheery. It smelled nice. It was fun to sit or lie on. If I spilled anything, I just scooped up the floor and threw it into the stove. The only disadvantages were a slight fire hazard and the fact that if you lost anything small, it was gone.

I lived in the house for four years. I only spent one winter there, mainly to field test it. The other three were spent out on the lecture circuit where it was possible to avoid "cabin fever," that dreaded winter plague of the North. One hundred and twenty square feet is not much living space, but due to economy of design things worked out nicely.

The front wall of the house, the one with thirteen windows facing the Uphill Patio, was eight feet high. This gave a guy room to walk around. Cooking was done in this area,

Left: Mike begins work on the lower wall of the $50 house.

The earth
is not his
brother,
but his
enemy, and
when he
has con-
quered it,
he moves
on.

Above: Mike stands in the doorway of the $50 under-ground house. Doorway leads out to Uphill Patio.

Below: View down through Uphill Patio and looking through wall of 13 windows into the house at dusk.

He leaves his father's graves behind and he does not care.

either standing around the stove or leaning out the barbecue windows (these, the fire-window, the PSP system and other features are all explained in later chapters). The other section of the house, where the ceiling came as low as three and one half feet, was for sitting and lying down activities. It was for writing, reading, playing the guitar, sleeping and other recreations.

When I first built the place I put three feet of earth on the roof. This was both to provide good growing conditions for vegetation and to meet government specifications for a fallout shelter. One morning, however, after several days of heavy rains, Willie Howitt, a hitchhiker who has spent many weeks helping me, and who was crashing there at the time, asked, "Did you hear that horrendous creak last night? It sounded like the whole house moved." Alarmed, I made a hasty inspection and discovered that it *had* moved. It had shifted down hill an inch or more throwing the plumb off the frame for the fire-window. I grabbed a shovel and went outside and took eighteen inches off the roof. Though the design was sound, my engineering was faulty for reasons we will examine in the chapter on construction.

The same poor engineering was responsible for another disaster; the east wall of the house began to push in. Though the north wall was uphill, the east wall was up-*ravine* and that ravine was exerting pressure no other wall of the house was subjected to. This left three choices: abandoning the house, repairing the damage, or adding another section to the east and using proper engineering. We chose the latter.

In the summer of 1975 we began work on what I've come to think of as a second house altogether, so radically did it change the function and appearance of the original $50 structure. We call it the $500 house.

Christopher Royer came out from Indiana to help. A bright, likeable architecture student, he wanted some first hand experience at underground construction. He got it—with a shovel in his hand.

We began by punching through a new

Wall begins pushing in due to poor engineering. Post at right (bark on) is an emergency support.

trail to the county road which corners my property nearly a half trail-mile away from the building site. Lynn Moore and I had back packed the millends over the 200 foot ridge which divides my property, but we needed a new system. A neighbor had given me some old 2x12 inch lumber up to eighteen feet long which he had salvaged by tearing down an abandoned saw mill. He wanted to get rid of the lumber to spruce up the property he was trying to sell. Did I want it? You bet I did. We skidded it by horse up the new trail.

After three weeks of hard digging we were ready to begin work on the structure itself. We set treated lodgepole pine posts in the ground and built the roofing beams and girders from tamarack, all of which was logged close to the site. When Chris finally left to go back east we had rebuilt some of the old house, had replaced a girder without disturbing the roof above, and had completed most of the structural work on the new section.

I worked on the house all that fall, winter and into the spring. The finished product was worth it. It has 370 square feet, is built on three levels, and includes a root cellar, 42 windows, white painted walls set off by stained and varnished posts and beams, and wall-to-wall carpeting (which alone was two-fifths the cost of the house).

Entrance to the house is now through a door in the "Royer Foyer." It is an excavation in the hillside. You enter from floor level terraces constructed on the downhill slope with the earth from the house excavation. There are no more stairs to climb up or down. Because of this and because there are so many windows, the most common reaction of bemused first-time visitors is, "But I thought the house was supposed to be underground!" It is. It's completely beneath the surface of the earth. "But I thought . . ." and here their voices trail off. "But you thought it was dark and windowless, like a cave, huh?"

"Well, yes."

Ha. The underground designer's moment of glory.

He kidnaps
the earth
from his
children.
He does not
care.

Seige-by-bear was common at the original $50 underground house when, during the early 1970's different bears respectively broke in through the firewindow, the barbecue windows, and the cooler. They, or others, also tore up a tent, tossed bedrolls around and hit a number of caches.

The author shot bears in 1972 and again in 1974—the first as the author stood on the roof, the second as the bear stood on the roof. That dissuaded them for years, so author was surprised on July 2, 1978 to see, entering the Uphill Patio, a bear displaying every intention of busting into house. Yells did not discourage him. A shot from an 8mm Mauser did.

"A ticklish moment," the author says. "They tend to run down hill when hit and this one was above me. I was ready to dive head first out the window, or to dash out the door in case he leaped, stumbled or rolled through the windows and down into the study. A wounded bear on your head is not a matter for levity."

Instead, the animal charged down through the patio, fell, got up prepared to charge again, and received a second shot through the spinal column which killed him several feet outside the window from which the author had been firing (shown closed in above photo). Terraces made it a simple one man operation to hang bear from extended roof girder in the patio barbecue area for gutting as shown at right (photo, Jim Hubbell).

With weeds knee high in garden, with hog pens needing building, with horse pasture fencing down, with a T.V. film crew due up in 48 hours to shoot house, author was now confronted with dead bear in patio hanging in heat which could soon spoil meat. Holding religious beliefs that one should use all of which one kills, author phoned local taxidermist to get help tanning hide, was persuaded to call game warden to get legal rights to animal killed out of season. Notified, game warden immediately confiscated bear, but promised meat would go to retirement home, hide would be salvaged. Game warden promptly buried bear—meat, hide, claws, all—for reasons author finds totally unacceptable.

Author did manage to hide heart and liver, both of which he promptly devoured. Since you-are-what-you-eat, author now—absurdly—claims he is a 175 lb. bear liver.

Above: Frances, an English hitchhiker friend who came for dinner, enjoys an early fire in the firewindow. Upper Right: Leaning through the barbecue windows, Mike lays birchbark tinder for a fire. Right: Study and bed area of the $50 house.

20

Wall of windows in the $50 Underground House face
Uphill Patio. Barbecue windows stand open, ready
for use.

His father's
graves and
his children's
birthright
are forgotten.

His appetite
will devour
the earth
and leave
behind only
a desert.

Mike and Frances wash Idaho potatoes for dinner.   Mike at typewriter.

Wall of windows. At top of stairway, Bummer I wears
chain to break him of chasing deer.

Frances reads by firewindow.

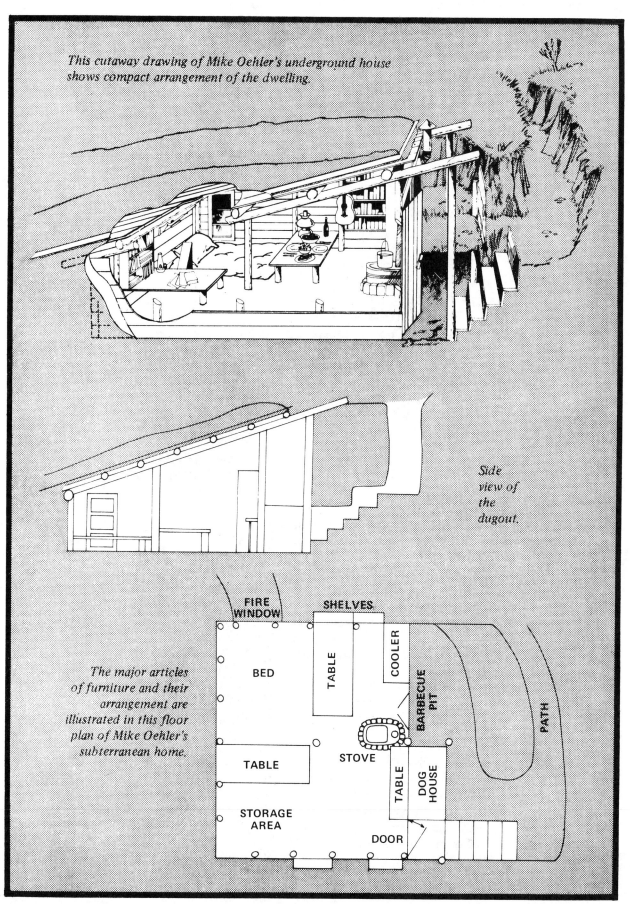

This cutaway drawing of Mike Oehler's underground house shows compact arrangement of the dwelling.

Side view of the dugout.

The major articles of furniture and their arrangement are illustrated in this floor plan of Mike Oehler's subterranean home.

FIRE
WINDOW

SHELVES

BED

TABLE

COOLER

BARBECUE PIT

TABLE

STOVE

PATH

TABLE

DOG HOUSE

STORAGE AREA

DOOR

Drawing courtesy *Lifestyle!* Magazine.

Chapter 4
THE PSP SYSTEM

PSP stands for Post/Shoring/Polyethylene. These are the materials and the system which we use for building our undergrounds in Northern Idaho and, increasingly, throughout the west. Because the materials are different from those used by underground architects in the east we think of our methods as the Western School of Underground Architecture.

The easterners use concrete as a basic building material. (We fondly think of the easterners as Concrete Terrorists.) The easterners use concrete because the resultant buildings will last for centuries avoiding disruption of the flora and fauna on the roof. Some like concrete because the roofs can withstand a greater load. They want to build places that can withstand the weight of trees.

We can't argue with these thoughts. It is certainly desirable to leave the vegetation on the roof undisturbed for centuries. And it is a testament to the degree of environmental concern of underground architects that they should insist upon roof soil conditions which allow the true natural environment and native trees to reassert themselves.

However . . .

(1) Cement is a non-renewable resource.
(2) Cement is rarely native to the building site. Being very heavy it takes great amounts of energy to transport.
(3) Concrete is too permanent. To knock out a wall or punch through a new window or work on the pipes beneath a slab floor one must rent a jack hammer or hire a crew at great expense.

(4) Concrete is lousy to look at. It has no soul.
(5) Concrete is expensive. Labor costs are high. There is more work (and material) involved in just building the forms for a pour than there is in building an entire wall by the PSP system.
(6) Concrete is a poor insulator. One inch of lumber is a better insulator than six inches of concrete. In many cases then concrete necessitates the additional expense of insulation.
(7) Concrete is difficult for the owner-builder to work with.

Wood is the basic component of the PSP system. Wood is fantastic stuff. Pound for pound it is stronger than steel. It is a renewable resource. It is abundant and can be found on many building sites. It is easily worked and can be milled on the site by the builder with a chainsaw and Alaskan Mill. Wood has warmth, richness and soul. It even smells good.

In the PSP system treated posts are set into the ground after the excavation has been made. Beams for the roof are notched into these. Then a sheet of polyethylene is stretched around the outside of the wall. Shoring is placed between the posts and the polyethylene, one board at a time. The polyethylene is stretched snug, and earth is back-filled behind, pressing the polyethylene against the shoring and the shoring against the posts.

The sight of your cities pains the eyes of the redman.

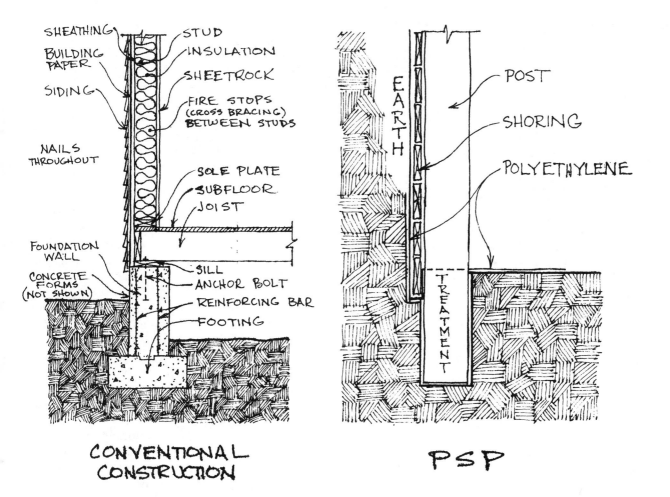

CONVENTIONAL CONSTRUCTION

Labels (left diagram):
- SHEATHING
- BUILDING PAPER
- SIDING
- STUD
- INSULATION
- SHEETROCK
- FIRE STOPS (CROSS BRACING) BETWEEN STUDS
- NAILS THROUGHOUT
- SOLE PLATE
- SUBFLOOR
- JOIST
- FOUNDATION WALL
- CONCRETE FORMS (NOT SHOWN)
- SILL
- ANCHOR BOLT
- REINFORCING BAR
- FOOTING

PSP

Labels (right diagram):
- EARTH
- POST
- SHORING
- POLYETHYLENE
- TREATMENT

We believe the PSP system is a real breakthrough. Less than half the materials are used than in, say, the construction of a frame house.

While wood is the basic component of the PSP system, polyethylene is the secret of its success. Polyethylene is inexpensive, easy to work with, and readily available. It is an absolute moisture barrier and is what keeps the wooden walls from rotting. While it is true that this plastic deteriorates quickly when exposed to the ultraviolet rays of sunlight, it lasts indefinitely underground. (Environmentalists are concerned that garbage buried in polyethylene bags may not decompose for centuries because it never becomes exposed to the dampness of the earth.) Being new to mankind this material has allowed us to develop a building system which is equally new.

Though polyethylene is an absolute moisture barrier, it is not fool proof: a small pinprick or tear could lead to really annoying leaks if the structure is not designed and constructed with this possibility in mind. Therefore, one cardinal rule of design must be followed: DESIGN SO THAT ALL WATER MAY FREELY RUN OFF OR AWAY FROM THE STRUCTURE. *Never* let the water back up against the house, for if you do, sooner or later it is going to find a way in.

The PSP system, being new, has had a field test of only six years at this writing, so we can make no absolute guarantees of duration. The individual components are expected to last well, however. As we've said polyethylene has a life expectancy of centuries underground. Posts treated with Penta were at first expected to last only thirty-five years out in the weather as fence posts. The industry has

But perhaps it is because the redman is a savage and does not understand ...

25

There is no quiet place in the white man's cities.

recently lengthened the expectancy to fifty years, and it may go higher. (Penta is also too new to have been field tested for a long period.) The wooden walls should last nearly as long as the polyethylene behind them. Wooden beams do well. There are wooden beams on old mill buildings in the eastern part of the country which are as sturdy after two hundred years as they were when they were installed. Some buildings in England are reported to have load-carrying beams four hundred years old.

The one weakness in the system, then, would appear to be the posts. Yet, if industry is guaranteeing the posts to last for fifty plus years out in the weather, we might reasonably expect them to last for seventy years or more in the shelter of a house where they are not exposed to rain and sun, freezing and thawing. And when they do rot out they may be replaced with a minimum of fuss and effort. They may be replaced individually causing no disturbance of the roof or earth, plants and animals above. The technique for replacement is discussed later.

THE EARTH/CARPET FLOOR

Aside from the prevailing prejudices against underground housing itself, there are few concepts which create more resistance than the thought of an earthen floor.

For good reason. Once the straw on the floor of my $50 underground house wore out, the dust began to rise creating a film over everything in the place. Earth is not so much fun to sit or lie on either. You feel, well . . . dirty.

Mexican women seem to solve this problem somewhat by sweeping water into the floor daily hardening or setting up the earth at least temporarily. Some folks in the southwest sweep linseed oil into their floors, wait a day or so, and repeat the process. Though still allowing "give" this sets the earth nearly like concrete; you can wipe up a dropped egg without getting any earth on the rag. Others go to more elaborate and artistic extents: they mix up adobe, pour it six inches thick on the floor, smooth it down, wait for days or weeks for it to dry and crack into the mosaic of dried mud, mix up another adobe mixture and fill in the cracks, wait for it to dry, sweep in linseed oil and wait for it to dry and then

repeat with linseed oil again. The resultant floor looks like tile, sets up like concrete yet still has give to the walker and will not poke through except when walked across by someone wearing spike high heel shoes or loggers calked boots. Even then, repair is as simple as mixing up a small adobe mixture and filling the holes.

Our own favorite flooring, bar none, however, is a simple earth/polyethylene/carpet floor.

We vastly prefer this over both concrete and wooden floors even when they are carpeted.

A concrete floor costs a lot of money to pour. It is cold and unpleasant to look at. If there are plumbing pipes, electrical conduits, or radiant heat tubes beneath, any malfunction is a disaster necessitating the hiring of a jackhammer crew and cement mason besides the repairman.

But the worst thing about a concrete floor is what it does to someone who has to walk on it all the time. As countless housewives, store clerks, and factory workers have learned to their sorrow, working continually on concrete floors usually results in varicose veins, fallen arches or other foot and leg disorders.

There is no give whatsoever to concrete.

To be continually pounding your feet and legs against an unyielding surface is only slightly less damaging than to be continually pounding your head, fists or other body parts against an unyielding surface. Duckboards, thick carpets, rubber mats and the like are often employed to help ease the situation but they are only sops. The problem is that concrete was used in the first place.

In recognition of this dilemma, wooden floors are built. There is a give to wooden floors which eliminates most of the varicose vein/fallen arch syndrome. However, wooden floors present a series of problems of their own. Consider:

Wooden floors are quite flammable. Burning objects have a way of falling, and if a wooden floor is what they fall upon it could be all over. Wooden floors should be regarded as fire hazards.

Wooden floors are noisy. At best they creak and groan. At worst, say when there are children playing on them in hard heeled shoes, they are intolerable. You might as well

26

have a herd of children tap dancing across a giant snare drum as have them playing on a wooden floor. Carpets help but do not eliminate the problem.

Wooden floors are expensive. First you have to set 2x6 or 2x8 joists, build cross bracing, lay subflooring, building paper and a good quality tongue-and-groove hardwood. You must drive nails everywhere. That's a lot of material and a lot of labor.

Wooden floors are subject to rot and to termite attack. For this reason, and because it is necessary to do something to make it possible to work on the pipes beneath without ripping out the floor each time something goes wrong, "crawl spaces" are built. (This is where there is no basement or where the house is not pole construction.)

Crawl spaces are just what their name implies—areas in which to crawl around under the wooden floor inspecting or spraying for termites, or to work on the plumbing or electrical systems. Crawl spaces also are constructed to allow circulation of air to inhibit rot in wooden floors caused by damp. This has the unfortunate effect of bringing cold air under the house in winter which makes the floors cold and further raises heating bills and wastes energy. It can also freeze the pipes.

Crawl spaces are usually constructed by raising the concrete footings of a house a couple of feet. This involves considerable expense in the shorings for the pour, re-bars and concrete, and, of course, labor.

Earth/polyethylene/carpet floors, however, circumvent all these problems. Though there is a certain amount of labor involved in smoothing out the earth before laying the carpets, it is less labor than is involved in making a pour. Getting at malfunctioning pipes and conduits is as simple as rolling up a carpet and layer of polyethylene and getting out a shovel. Aside from the cost of polyethylene and carpet, this floor is dirt cheap.

Yet the greatest benefit is how the earth treats your feet and legs. It treats them beautifully. It treats them as though you were strolling in a grassy meadow. Your feet and legs were *designed* to walk on earth. No one will ever improve upon earth as a composition for the health and comfort of the lower extremities.

The earth/carpet floor is relatively fireproof. It is silent to the tread. It does away with all of the crawl space expense and hassle. The pipes, buried snugly in the womb of the earth, will never freeze. The floor stays warm, drawing upon the geothermal energies. With the polyethylene barrier protecting the carpet, this floor cannot rot. Termites are never a problem.

Some consider the earth/polyethylene/carpet flooring the finest available to man.

No place to hear the leaves of spring or the rustle of insect's wings.

Chapter 5
DESIGN

You MUST have a good design if you are to build a fully livable house. Please do not think that you can sink a box into the ground and let it go at that. There is much more to it. Even many of the trained architects building underground today are botching the job so pay close attention. Since you will have to live with your design strengths and weaknesses daily for years, or perhaps the rest of your life, this chapter on design is the most important part of the book for you.

First off, we will be dealing primarily with underground houses on hillsides. Hillsides are preferred building sites for a number of reasons. For one, the drainage is better. For another, you stand a better chance of getting a sweeping view. Still another is that hilly land is traditionally less expensive than flat land, and it is what most back-to-the-landers usually wind up with. Sewage disposal is greatly simplified when there is indoor plumbing. Then there are the terrain advantages of building on the warm, sunny south slopes in cold climates and on the cooler northern slopes in hot climates. Finally, and perhaps most importantly, flat land is usually prime agricultural land and should be left as such.

This is not to turn you off if all you have is flat land or if, for whatever reason, your best building site is in a flat area. If you must build there by all means build underground. Unless the flat land is swampy, poorly drained, or has little soil above bedrock, there is no reason a U house won't work. We'll present some designs later in the chapter which are applicable to flat areas. Hillsides are just *better* building sites, whether the house is below or above ground, that's all.

Aside from choosing the site itself, there are three major points of consideration when designing a U house. These are (1) drainage, (2) windows and view, and (3) the living area and features. Of the three drainage is by far the most important. It is the one you have to whip *first* before you can begin to consider the others. A house that leaks is a house that fails.

FIRST-THOUGHT HOUSE

Right here, before going any further, we will eliminate what, for lack of a better name, I call the First-Thought House. I call it this because it is the design that 99 per cent of the

but perhaps because I am a savage and do not understand the clatter only seems to insult the ears.

people think of first when considering an underground house on a hillside. It is the design that I considered first myself. Fortunately, there was a six month wait between my decision to go underground and the actual start of construction and in the interim I was able to think my way clear.

The First-Thought House is an attempt to get a view downhill at the expense of the primary consideration, drainage. Drainage, in fact, is sometimes never considered at all. The design consists of a large wall of windows on the downhill side and a shed roof which drains back against the hillside. A cutaway view of the First-Thought House looks like this:

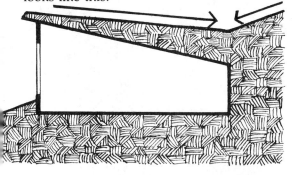

There are five problems which the First-Thought House creates. First of all, since there are no windows on the uphill side, there is no way to achieve a balance of light. Everything facing the downhill windows will be bright and everything facing that blank back wall will be dark and shadowy. Having the windows all on one side creates a second problem in trying to get cross ventilation. To get a breeze through the house with this design a guy would pretty near have to build air scoops (like the funnels on ships). But why? Wouldn't it be better to put some windows on that uphill side?

A third potentially serious problem is created because the entrances must all be on the same side of the house. This is dangerous. In case of fire, cave-in, or attack you are trapped. Few burrowing animals are satisfied with one entrance. It is an instinctive thing with them and it will be with you, too. You just won't feel *right* with all of the entrances on one side of the house. Your building inspector probably will not feel right either.

Having an exit on the opposite side can save your life as it may have done with yr. author on one of several occasions when bears broke into his house.

A fourth difficulty which is created by the First-Thought design is that it makes no allowance for lateral thrust, a problem which is aggravated by hillsides and/or wet earth. Lateral thrust is the pressure which is exerted against the walls of an underground house. (Some soils exert more than others. Sand is bad, loose gravel is worse, and oozy clay exerts the most pressure of all.) Hillsides move. They creep like glaciers. Woe to the guy who designs while ignoring this factor. In a few years your house may be literally bent out of shape. The walls may be pushed in. By putting windows and a patio on the uphill side as in the Basic Design discussed below, the effects of lateral thrust and hillside creep are lessened and in some cases completely eliminated.

The final, and perhaps greatest, mistake of the First-Thought design is one of drainage. What happens to the water coming down the hill? In most cases no provision is made to take care of it. What happens to the precipitation which falls on the roof? It flows back to join the water coming down the hill. All of that water is going to gang up on you against the back wall. Sooner or later, one way or another, that water is going to find its way through or under the wall no matter what water proofing techniques you use. I have seen it happen. I have seen it happen to very expensive underground structures.

I won't deny that you can get an excellent view with the First-Thought design. And it is a temptation in this, the dawning of the age of solar energy, to face all of those windows to the south to make maximum use of the sun. HOWEVER, those same effects can be achieved by other means without the problems encountered with this design. To reiterate, this design causes five heavy problems. These are: (1) No balance of light; (2) No cross-ventilation; (3) Entrances are all on one side of the house creating a potential trap; (4) No allowance for lateral thrust and hillside creep; and (5) Anticipated disastrous drainage problems.

And what is there to life if a man cannot hear the lovely cry of a whippoorwill or the arguments of the frogs around the pond at night?

THE BASIC DESIGN

If not the First-Thought House, what then is a design which is suitable for hillside underground construction? We offer the Basic Design, the design of the original $50 underground house and of all our subsequent hillside work. It's a design of proven success.

The Basic Design consists of two things: (1) a shed roof house with many windows which face (2) an excavated patio on the uphill side. It looks like this:

INVITES ELEVATION CHANGES WITHIN A HOUSE. Elevation changes within a room or between rooms can be of distinct advantage in a house. We've devoted a special section to this later. A shed roof is the perfect roof to have over head in such circumstances. It invites these elevation changes.

ADDS INTEREST. Why do we spend most of our lives in squares and rectangles? A shed roof (therefore a slanted ceiling) adds interest and character to any room. It breaks the old patterns.

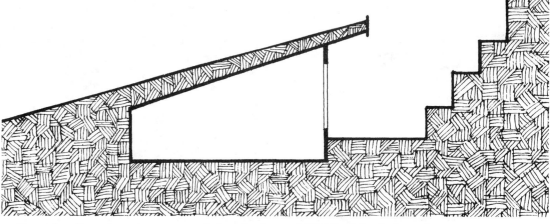

Consider first the advantages of the shed roof:

DRAINAGE. All the precipitation which lands on the roof has a natural run-off down the hill and away from the house. It never gets a chance to back up against the uphill wall where it would surely leak through. It doesn't even flow off to the sides of the house where it could cause mischief. Instead, it flows downhill away from the house where it can present no problems.

EASE OF CONSTRUCTION. The shed type roof is the easiest of all to construct. It is simplicity itself. Twelve-year-old boys could construct this sort of roof. Many have, in fact, on their forts and tree houses. This means that any owner-builder can do the same no matter how inexperienced or incompetent. When built by a professional crew it means less labor costs.

FOLLOWS THE NATURAL CONTOUR OF THE HILL. The shed roof can and should follow the pitch of the hill (with the possible exception of where the hill is so steep as to cause problems). This makes the house blend in with the hill as all good houses do. It is an aesthetic plus.

HELPS TO DISTRIBUTE HEAT. Many back-to-the-lander owner/built houses do not have central heat, but rely instead on one or two stoves. Elevation changes and a shed roof will distribute the heat much more effectively than is the case with a flat roof/single elevation home (assuming, of course, that the stoves are put in the lower section).

Now consider the advantages of the Uphill Patio. There are ten of them. They are:
(1) DRAINAGE.
(2) LATERAL THRUST.
(3) EMERGENCY EXIT.
(4) AESTHETIC REASONS.
(5) GREENHOUSE.
(6) ENERGY SAVINGS.
(7) BARBECUE WINDOWS.
(8) VIEW.
(9) BALANCE OF LIGHT.
(10) CROSS VENTILATION.

Your number one problem on underground housing is DRAINAGE. As mentioned, the shed roof on our Basic Design effortlessly disposes of all precipitation that falls on the roof. But what about the water coming down the hill? The patio takes care of that.

The Indian prefers the soft sound of the wind darting over the face of the pond, and the smell of the wind itself cleansed by a mid-day rain,

30

The Uphill Patio allows water coming down the hill to soak into the earth below floor level before reaching the house. In areas of poorly draining soils, such as those with high clay content, a "French-drain" (trench filled with gravel or crushed rock) or other special drainage provision should be used in the patio and along the side walls. On the original $50 and $500 houses this has never been necessary. Though our part of Idaho is influenced by West Coast weather patterns, and I have experienced twenty-eight days of rain in one month, the Basic Design has done its work and kept the house from flooding. Sure, there was a little difficulty in the beginning with water flowing down a stairway to the lowest point in the patio, the point just outside the door. I temporarily solved the problem by digging a hole and bailing it out several times a day. Now I've removed the stairs and have deepened the hole to hit a layer of sand which drains the water away effortlessly. No more problems whatsoever. So . . . it may be said that the Basic Design will solve most drainage problems and that the Basic Design/French drain combination should solve all others.

LATERAL THRUST, as previously mentioned, is the pressure exerted by the earth. Hillside creep is a hill itself slowly responding to gravity. We have seen how this effect may push in a wall or even bend a whole house out of shape. But not when there is an Uphill Patio.

The Uphill Patio eliminates the lateral thrust of hillside creep by eliminating the hillside itself—at least for some feet above the house. There can be no pressure if there is no hillside to exert it. True, the hillside must be shored up, and the shoring may in time push in, but it is far easier to repair shoring outside than the wall of a house.

Then too, the uphill shoring may be integrated with the frame of the house by means of braces. This may seem to be self defeating, that it puts the pressure back on the house, but consider: whereas with the First-Thought House there is nothing to counteract the pressure from the hill, with the Basic Design there is solid earth on the downhill side. If the hillside pushes from above it must push against the hillside below and the whole house will move with the hill without complication, the way a buried log might.

The First-Thought House may possibly inch further out of the ground, bend out of shape, or just cave in at the pressure point.

An EMERGENCY EXIT, or second entrance, is possible with the Basic Design. It opens onto the Uphill Patio. It is only a secondary entrance here because one must climb up or down when using it. Where is the main entrance? Through the Royer Foyer or the gable where one may enter at floor level without stairs at all. Remember that the Basic Design is only *Basic*; there are other design features to be added.

The AESTHETIC REASONS for having an Uphill Patio, besides the fact that the patio is a thing of beauty itself being mostly garden, is that the windows are invisible to anyone other than those who are standing directly above the patio. In other words, the windows are not visible by neighbors either on the same slope, in the valley below, or from a possible opposing hillside. This should be of prime consideration where there is a high density of housing.

A GREENHOUSE can and should be constructed from the Uphill Patio. Cover the patio over with corrugated plastic, clear fiberglass, or tempered glass (remember things are prone to walk over surfaces which are at ground level) and you have one of the finest greenhouses imaginable. The perhaps 50 degrees radiating from the earth, the sun's energy being trapped beneath the fiberglass, and the heat loss from the windows of the house should keep that greenhouse warm without additional heat. By covering the greenhouse at night and cracking a window the plants should survive even the coldest temperatures.

or scented with a piñon pine.

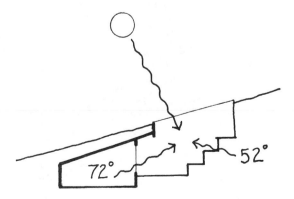

Where the uphill patio is not converted into a greenhouse it still saves energy by sheltering the windows from the worst of the wind. Houses, like people, are subject to a chill factor of the wind. Windows especially, since they lose as much as fifteen times the amount of heat as does a well insulated wall. The higher the wind the greater the heat loss. The Uphill Patio makes sheltered windows possible.

The last four benefits—barbecue windows, views, cross ventilation, and balance of light—will be covered in later sections.

The next four sections deal with posts and elevation changes and their special uses—features which are either common to or unique with underground housing.

Posts

Who wants posts in the middle of the room? No one. They interfere with traffic, view, continuity of the room and are sure to be bumped into in unwary moments.

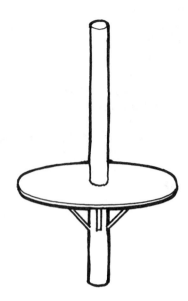

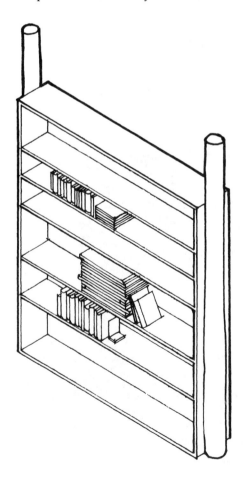

So you will try to design with most or all of your posts along the walls. In some cases this may mean putting in an extra beam or two. In other cases it may mean designing the room a little longer and narrower than you otherwise might. Or it might mean dividing a room into several elevations and using posts as shoring retainers at the elevation change.

Posts along the walls can have three or more functions. In the corner of a room they can not only provide roof support but could be shoring retainers for both east/west and north/south walls and possibly the jamb for either a door, window, or closet besides.

Remember that your posts are things of beauty. They are not cold concrete columns in a parking lot supporting the tier above, nor are they some monstrous pillar painted a pathetic pastel which carries the burden of six floors of department store junk over your head. Instead they support living soil and vegetation. They are trees which needed thinning, cut so that others might grow better. Hopefully they were from your own building site and have been lovingly hand-worked to bring out the grain and insect markings. Varnished and perhaps stained, they become works of art.

But you can still bump into works of art. Sometimes you may need to design with posts in the center of the room. Don't despair. Multiple use may be made of these posts, also.

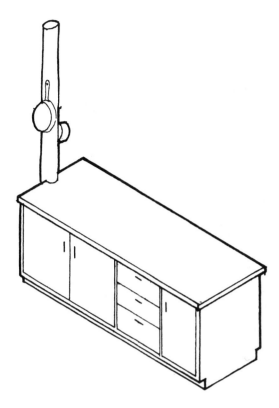

One such center post in my house serves in seven capacities. They are: (1) Roof support; (2) Psychological assurance of strength; (3) Psychological divider of one section of the house from another; (4) Retainer for the north/south shoring of a mini-level; (5) Retainer for the east/west shoring of the same mini-level; (6) Visual reminder that there is a mini-level so that you do not trip; and (7) Something to grab onto in case you trip anyway.

There are other uses you may put to posts in the middle of a room. If it is a single post you might want to make it the center support of a round table. Such a table will certainly never wobble because the leg was unstable. Or you could use it as the end support of a work counter or book case, or for a stack of cabinets.

Two or more posts can be used as both ends of tables, bookshelves, counters or cabinet stacks. Cleverly placed these items will add to the utility of the room by channeling the flow of traffic, providing quiet nooks, or serving as function separators (physical barriers within a room which serve to delineate space used for one function from space used for another—e.g., bookshelves separating a TV area from reading or conver-

sation areas). In addition, posts may be used to hang lanterns, lamps, coats, artwork, clotheslines or other items.

Don't design with posts in the living area of a room if you can avoid it, but if you can't avoid it, make full use of the ones you must have.

Elevation Changes

Since we are dealing mainly with houses on hillsides, attention must be paid to elevational differences both between rooms and within the rooms themselves.

As with the case of having roof-supporting posts in a house, having elevational changes may be viewed as either a detriment or as a bonus. Those who think of it as a detriment will bewail the fact that they must climb stairs. Those who recognize it as a bonus realize that elevational differences add character to a house; help separate various areas for different functions; help distribute heat in homes without central heating; and make it possible to have spectacular views through the use of clerestories. They also make possible some interesting special features.

For all things share the same breath~ the beasts, the trees, the man.

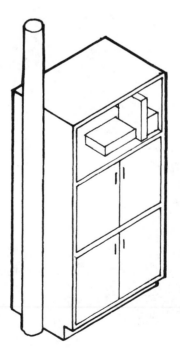

33

The white man does not seem to notice the air he breathes.

In my $500 house the elevational differences within the essentially one room structure came about for a more pragmatic reason than any of the above: it saved us considerable digging. (It was entirely hand dug, you'll recall.) Yet three of the above benefits became apparent very quickly: the house was much more interesting than it would have been had it been one level; the heat rose to make the study/bedroom (where the least physical exertion occurred) the warmest part of the house though it was the furthest away from the stove; and it made the three sections of the house both psychologically and physically separate by function while allowing visual sweep, air circulation and balance of light.

Had it not been for the four foot elevation rise of the study/bedroom, the north wall of that area would have been nearly twelve feet from floor to ceiling making it a most uninteresting dark and difficult wall to liven up. It would have also added four more feet of potential drainage problems since with its existing six foot rise from floor to windows it already comes close to violating our cardinal rule of not allowing the drainage to back up against a wall.

I don't think, as a designer, I'd particularly go out of my way to add elevational differences on a house built on a flat area. I suspect that could look a little contrived unless one were making use of the clerestory concept—but I surely would work with the idea on a hillside home.

Be wary of elevational differences within a room of heavy use such as the kitchen. You don't want to be climbing up and stumbling down stairs in a work area.

Be wary also of elevational differences between rooms of related use such as the kitchen and dining rooms for the same reasons.

ELEVATION CHANGES: SPECIAL FEATURES

One of the interesting uses for an elevation change is the table/seat concept. A person may sit on the upper tier and dangle his legs down into the elevation below while dining, writing or whatever at a table specially constructed in the lower elevations to meet these needs. Portable back rests may be used if desired. People may sit at the other side of the table on conventional stools or chairs.

Photo at left shows post with seven functions. An elevation change is seen in midpicture with a mini-level at lower right.

34

A variation of this theme is to mold seats with backrests right into the elevation change itself. These may be to service a table such as the dining room table, or they may be simply a row of seats, or they may be built as an "L" or "U" shaped conversation pit.

TO KEEP CHILDREN, PETS, DRUNKS, ETC. from falling off, a desk, work bench, bookcase, home entertainment console, bar or other feature may be built along the upper edge of the elevation change. This would also serve as both a sight and sound barrier to separate the activities at each elevation while still allowing clerestory views, light balance, and cross ventilation.

MINI-LEVELS

Mini-levels divide one elevation of the house or room from another. They primarily function as stairs but can have these advantages:

(1) They are aesthetically pleasing and add character to a room;

(2) They gentle one elevation into another;

(3) They are safer than stairs, making the change less abrupt. If a guy trips going down there are a few feet in which to catch the balance, not another stair immediately to further mess him up.

(4) They are forever being used as seats. They seem to function, in fact, as miniature conversation pits.

Excellent storage areas may be constructed beneath mini-levels. Built carefully, these areas can become secret compartments with a piece of carpet on top covering the trap door.

A person would probably want to stick with stairs in out of the way places, or where there is considerable elevation to be overcome, or where space is crucial. Otherwise mini-levels can be highly interesting.

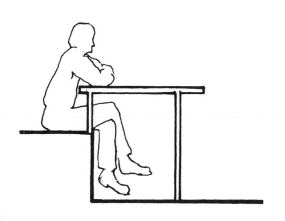

Drawings show table/seat concept at elevation changes. Top drawing has seat built into earth itself, plus a desk above to keep things from falling off.

Photo shows the three elevation changes within the $500 house. Highest level (study area) in foreground, middle level (guitar) in center and lowest level (stove) on left.

Like a man dying for many days, he is numb to the stench.

35

If I decide to accept, I will make one condition. The white man must treat the beasts of this land as his brothers.

VIEWS, LIGHT AND VENTILATION

There are five approved methods of getting good views and lots of light and air into the underground house. These are:

(1) The Uphill Patio concept of the Basic Design.
(2) The Offset Room.
(3) Clerestories.
(4) The Royer Foyer.
(5) Gables.

Using the methods of building favored by the easterners there are four additional methods of getting light and air into a house, though not always a view. These methods are:

(1) The First-Thought design.
(2) Atriums.
(3) Skylights.
(4) Lightwells.

Five Approved Methods of Design

THE UPHILL PATIO

We have seen how the Uphill Patio solves the problems of drainage and lateral thrust, how it functions as an emergency exit or second entrance, how it adds to the aesthetic appeal of a given neighborhood, and why it makes the perfect greenhouse and promotes energy savings.

Now we'll see how the Uphill Patio allows a good view, a balance of light, and cross ventilation.

Remember first that on the designs of most underground houses today the wall against the hill is solid with no windows. A few of the architects are sinking costly light wells, and some are advocating wind scoops, but these are single function features. Such features don't come within a mile of the ten benefits of the Uphill Patio. They don't even come within a hundred yards of providing balance of light, cross ventilation, and a good view, all three at once.

A balance of light is desirable to keep things from looking dark and shadowy on one side, and to keep one part of a given room from being dingy. It also cuts electrical or kerosene bills and promotes energy savings. It makes a room much more cheery to have light coming in from at least two sides.

Cross ventilation is desirable to clear wood smoke out of the air, to whisk away cooking odors and other possibly objectionable smells, to provide a cooling breeze, and in the evening, to dry up the dampness which sometimes occurs inside on hot summer days. (Warm, moisture laden summer air coming in contact with the cool walls of an underground structure creates a minor condensation "problem"; the walls feel clammy. In the winter, however, the high humidity of some underground houses is a distinct healthy plus.)

The Uphill Patio cannot provide balance of light and cross ventilation all by itself, of course. These are only possible when other windows and doors are added through incorporation of Royer Foyers, Offset Rooms, clerestories or gables. The Uphill Patio can, however, give us a unique view by itself.

The Uphill Patio can give us what we call a *controlled view*. That is, a view that can be altered only by consent of the owner of the house. Which is to say, no matter what things neighbors or business or governments construct nearby, they can't ruin your view. Because that view—of the Uphill Patio—is of a garden you've planted yourself bounded by walls you've constructed yourself.

The deeper your windows and the narrower and shorter the patio, the more protected your view, or, to put it another way, the higher the trajectory of sight. This means that the deeper, shorter, narrower the Uphill Patio, the higher and closer to your property lines your neighbors may build without your being forced to view whatever it is that they have constructed.

Obversely, the more protected the view the more restricted it is. Panoramic sweeps—unless mirrors are used—are possible only of the sky. But that's all right. Those wide sweeping views may be obtained by other means; by clerestories, by Royer Foyers or by gables. The challenge here it to make full use of that Uphill Patio.

The Japanese have been making use of restricted view areas for centuries and have been doing a magnificent job of it. Their rock gardens, created within the confines of a courtyard are recognized the world around as works of art. This ability to create beauty in the smallest of areas elicits the admiration of gardeners and landscapers everywhere. Your Uphill Patio might too if you put some effort into it.

Again, we hope that the walls of the patio are of PSP rather than concrete. Concrete is cold and impersonal, while the posts and shoring have warmth and character. Knot holes and the grains of the wood should add interest to, rather than detract from, the beauty of the patio. With wood it is also easy to drive nails, eyelets, holders and so forth to aid the climbing or hanging plants.

Your patio wall should consist of mini-terraces or "steps back" anywhere from a few inches to a number of feet in depth. These should be planted with a mixture of things: flowers, shrubs, vegetables, hanging plants, climbing plants, vines, ivy, or whatever the gardener can conjure up.

Remember to plant plenty of climbing or hanging varieties to cover those wall spaces. What ever happened to vertical greenery in the United States? Even the Ivy League colleges have little ivy on the walls anymore. Yet a wall can be a beautiful, flowering, air purifying, oxygen producing, wildlife sheltering, living surface too, if anyone takes the effort to make it so.

The lowest terrace of the patio itself (as opposed to the patio walls) may or may not be devoted to outdoor living space. It makes a dandy barbecue area, eating or lounging area. If used as such it should probably reflect the mode of decor of the interior. This helps to make the transition from interior to exterior. It helps to bring the outdoors indoors, as it were. If the walls of the interior are white (as suggested) then this part of the patio should probably have white walls, too. White walls are particularly desirable in the lowest reaches of the patio where light is dimmest. Any aid here which will help to reflect light through the windows and into the house should be used.

Because sunlight may rarely, if ever, penetrate to the lowest reaches of the patio, rocks, weathered, or gnarled pieces of wood or driftwood should probably play an important part of your garden there. Ferns grow well without much sunlight and look handsome among such inanimate natural art objects. The middle terraces of the patio might best be planted to bright flowers which thrive in partial shade. The highest, sunniest, and least

visible terraces, might best be suited for your vegetable crops. The vertical walls, as we have said, should be profuse with hanging or climbing vegetation, even if it does cut down somewhat on light reflection.

Drawing below illustrates Uphill Patio, barbecue windows and use of patio barbecue area. Two possible uses of mirrors are also indicated: To reflect sunlight into house through north windows, and to obtain view downhill over roof of house. (Special note by author: Drawing originally depicted man holding cup, woman about to pour tea. Drawing was made in Western Massachusetts, snakepit of Womens Liberation Movement, where it was declared that for wife to pour husband cup of tea was exploitive and degrading. Surreptitious and unauthorized change was made in drawing (fry pan substituted for cup), not to be discovered till author was thousand miles away. Change was intended to make it appear husband was helping to cook meal. More accurately reflecting current attitudes than impulsive young illustrator could have guessed, drawing actually now depicts vindictive Liberated Woman, behind husband's back, about to pour tea into fry pan.

I am a savage and I do not understand any other way.

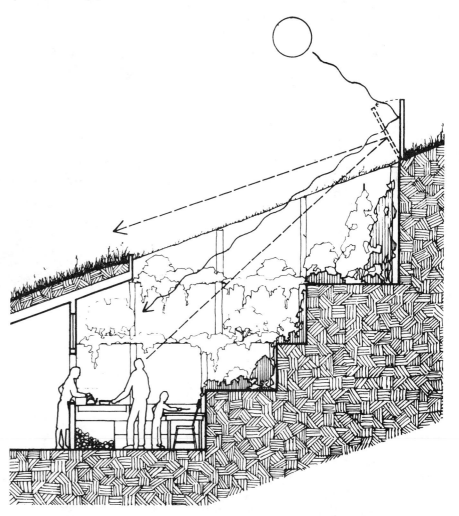

37

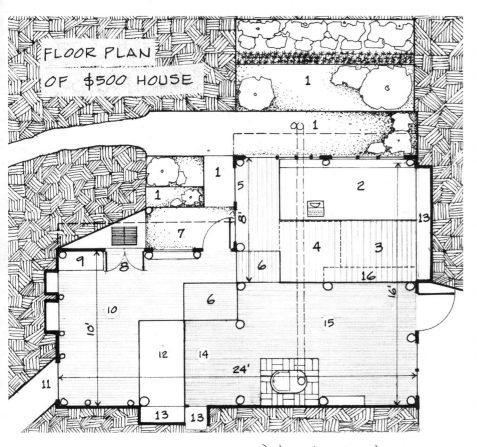

FLOOR PLAN
OF $500 HOUSE

There is one other eventuality which we haven't covered here: despite your best design efforts your "controlled view" out the patio could become marred. Neighbors could build a twenty story highrise one foot off your property line. Or the electric company might string a high voltage forest overhead. Or wishing the widest, shallowest, longest sunken patio possible, you might even build with a view of someone's ugly edifice visible from the start. What then? The answer here may be to keep the greenhouse covering over the patio year-round creating an artificial sky which blocks the offending structures from view. You will have to design so that on warm days the trapped heat may escape (if you do not have some way of capturing and storing it), but then you will have to design for this to have a fully functional greenhouse anyway. There may be one additional benefit from this year round greenhouse: as the atmospheric pollution continues to grow, your greenhouse attached to your dwelling is a way of filtering and purifying the domestic air you breathe.

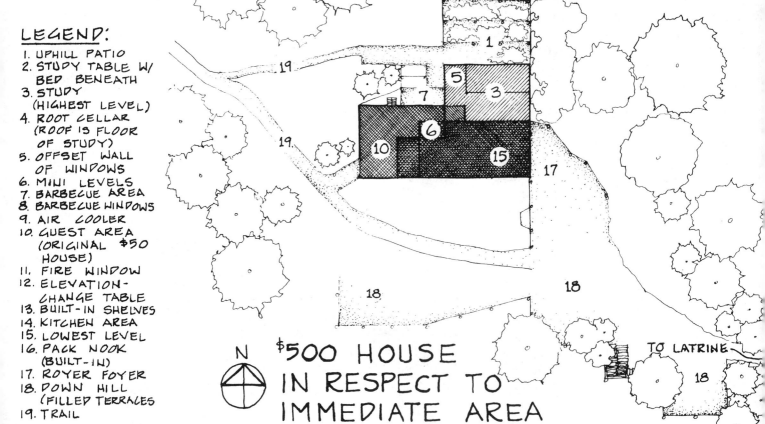

LEGEND:
1. UPHILL PATIO
2. STUDY TABLE W/ BED BENEATH
3. STUDY (HIGHEST LEVEL)
4. ROOT CELLAR (ROOF IS FLOOR OF STUDY)
5. OFFSET WALL OF WINDOWS
6. MINI LEVELS
7. BARBECUE AREA
8. BARBECUE WINDOWS
9. AIR COOLER
10. GUEST AREA (ORIGINAL $50 HOUSE)
11. FIRE WINDOW
12. ELEVATION-CHANGE TABLE
13. BUILT-IN SHELVES
14. KITCHEN AREA
15. LOWEST LEVEL
16. PACK NOOK (BUILT-IN)
17. ROYER FOYER
18. DOWN HILL (FILLED TERRACES)
19. TRAIL

N $500 HOUSE IN RESPECT TO IMMEDIATE AREA

TO LATRINE

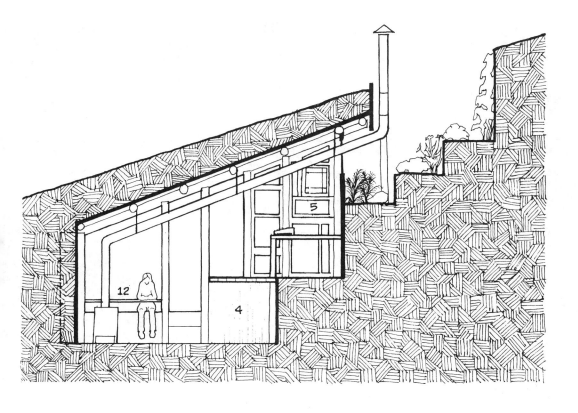

CROSS SECTION
OF $500 HOUSE,
NUMBERED TO
SHOW FEATURES.
REFER TO LEGEND
ON FACING
PAGE.

PHOTO SHOWS
UPHILL PATIO
AND OFFSET
WALL WINDOWS.

I have seen a thousand rotting buffalos on the prairies, left by the white man who shot them from a passing train.

Study Area.

Elevation change table, kitchen area and (background)
Royer Foyer.

Royer Foyer and lowest level.

Lowest level, stove and kitchen area.

THE OFFSET ROOM

By offsetting a second room so that it protrudes into the Uphill Patio you may get a whole section of windows which face a new direction altogether. There are a number of advantages to doing this.

First, you have the same advantages of a controlled view that you have with the Uphill Patio. Nothing that your neighbors construct is likely to be visible from the windows in the Offset section.

Secondly, you get the effect of a "second garden" for the price and effort of the first. This is to say that, though the windows of the Offset wall face the same Uphill Patio garden, they do so from a new direction and elevation making the garden appear different from the fresh perspective. Yet these benefits are accrued with no additional labor on your part; the excavation has already been made, the shoring put in place, the soil enriched, the plants grown and the rocks and other inanimate objects gathered and placed.

If the Offset Room is a higher elevation than the first room—as is the case with the study/bedroom in the $500 house—there is the additional esoteric benefit of being able to lie in bed and look out through windows at an evening "camp fire" in the barbecue area.

A third benefit of the Offset window section is that it allows light to enter the house from a new point of the compass. If the Uphill Patio is to the north of the house this means the Offset windows face either east or west allowing either the morning or evening sunlight to enter.

The fourth and fifth benefits to be gained by the Offset Room are balance of light and cross ventilation. The Offset Room will, of course, have its own Uphill Patio (since this is a nearly inviolable principle of design) and partial cross ventilation and balance of light may be achieved there. Both these effects will be complete when the Offset section is balanced by a Royer Foyer in the opposite corner of the room.

Photo shows wall of windows in Offset Room (author's study, $500 house) facing patio barbecue area and other parts of the Uphill Patio. Yr. author sleeps under the table in foreground to save space and to benefit from the best reading light in the house. At night he has a view out the lowest clear window to the fire in the barbecue cooking area. Translucent panels are "clear" fiberglass used both to fill awkward gaps and to allow light to enter home.

I am a savage and I do not understand how the smoking iron horse can be more important

THE ROYER FOYER

The Royer Foyer is a design invention which allows us to have a good view down a hill without rechanneling the flow of drainage or interrupting the purity of design of a shed roof. The Royer Foyer sneaks into the hillside rather than protruding from it. It makes possible a downhill view from windows that are all but concealed from neighbors.

The Royer Foyer is constructed by excavating a pie-shaped slice away from the house on a down side corner. This excavation is made from the side of the house, not from the true downhill wall as is the case with the First-Thought design. The excavation is pie shaped rather than perpendicular to the wall to allow flow of drainage so that no water is tempted to back up against either the house wall or the wall of the shoring of the foyer. If painted white the shoring wall acts as a light reflector throwing brilliant light into the house on sunny days during hours when bright sunlight might not otherwise enter.

When designed in conjunction with either clerestories or Offset Rooms in which the windows face the opposite direction of those of the foyer, or in conjunction with nearly any Uphill Patio, the Royer Foyer provides excellent balance of light and cross ventilation. Being set into the ground below true earth level the foyer is semi-sheltered from the winds. This lessens the amount of heat lost (chill factor) since the strongest winds cannot buffet the windows and doors, working their way through any available cracks.

Cover the open parts of the foyer with corrugated plastic or fiberglass and you have an automatic greenhouse much like the Uphill Patio greenhouse. The geothermal heat radiation from the floor and from the retaining wall, the heat loss from the windows and door, and the trapping of the sun's energy during the day should provide enough energy to keep the greenhouse warm during all but the extreme cold months. Even then, certain crops such as lettuce, cabbage, Brussels sprouts, kale and most of the root crops

might survive without any supplemental source of energy. If you were really intent on saving a delicate crop, such as tomatoes, during a cold spell, you could consider firing up the stove in the house a little more and cracking open the door. You might also consider throwing a tarp or hay or other insulator over the top at night. The retaining wall, if constructed of stone, could make an excellent heat retainer. A large stand up water tank lining that wall or fifty-five gallon water filled drums painted black could do the same. Again, as with the Uphill Patio, the foyer greenhouse should actually *save* you energy by keeping the heat down over your doors and windows much like stormwindows.

The Royer Foyer offers a fine view downhill even if at somewhat of an oblique angle. In the wintertime even when it is a greenhouse it provides a refreshing view as opposed to the sometimes bleak winter landscape; how nice to look out the window and see green growing plants rather than foreboding winter skies. In much of the northern United States people cover their windows in the winter with an outside layer of clear polyethylene which serves nicely as storm windows, and lets through the light, but which always blurs the view. Better, we think, to look at a lovingly tended greenhouse garden than polyethylene.

There is one more real advantage to the Royer Foyer; through it you may enter your underground house without climbing up or down stairs. When you excavate the foyer just excavate at the same level as the floor of the house. Use the excess earth to build downhill terraces the same level.

Top photo: View out Royer Foyer (from author's bed.)
Bottom photo: Royer Foyer from outside.

than the buffalo that we kill only to stay alive.

CLERESTORIES

Clerestories are nothing new to architecture. They are, in fact, a common design feature. I haven't seen them used yet by other underground designers, but they will be. They are a natural.

Clerestories, as we use them, are when one roof section is elevated above another and the space created between is given to windows. Usually this is between rooms but it need not always be so. It may be within a room also. If you have difficulty in visualizing the concept think of the caboose on a train. The windows that look out from the cupola down the length of the caboose are clerestory windows.

The clerestory concept allows us to add windows to a shed roof without interrupting the drainage, yet to keep the purity of design. The clerestory must go up and down the roof, of course, not across it.

Where clerestories are most exciting is where they are used in conjunction with elevation changes within a house. If there are two or more rooms which rise in elevation, and those rooms are separated from the others only by elevation changes and posts so that the effect is a flowing one—one room flows into another—it becomes possible then to sit in the room of highest elevation and look at eye level or down outside through the clerestory windows in the other rooms.

When built with an overhanging roof of several feet and two thicknesses of glass, one on the inside, one on the outside edge of the overhang, it becomes possible to create a mini greenhouse in the insulated airspace. All of the windows and doorways in the five approved methods of design offer greenhouse possibilities.

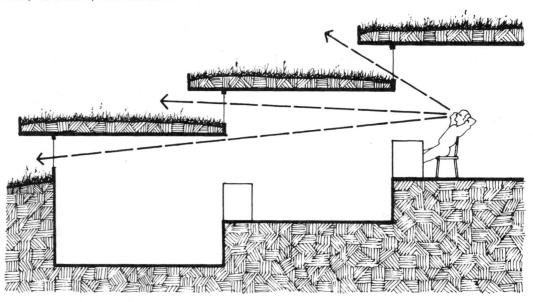

Above: The clerestory concept.

Left: Winter weather panels can turn clerestories into mini-greenhouses. When not needed, outer glass panels may be stored above growing surface. Inner panels should open like any other windows.

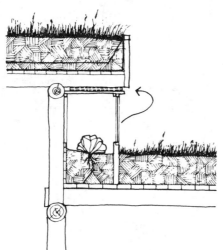

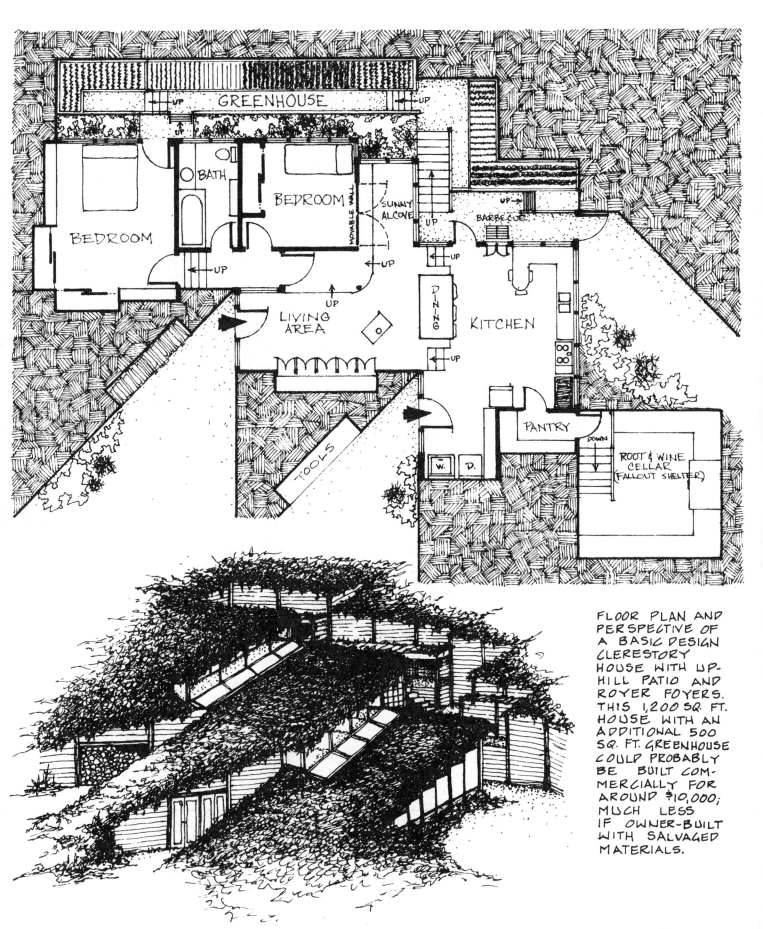

GREENHOUSE

BEDROOM

BATH

BEDROOM

MOVABLE WALL

SUNNY ALCOVE

UP

UP

UP

UP

UP

BARBECUE

UP

DINING

KITCHEN

LIVING AREA

UP

TOOLS

UP

PANTRY

W.   D.

DOWN

ROOT & WINE CELLAR (FALLOUT SHELTER)

FLOOR PLAN AND PERSPECTIVE OF A BASIC DESIGN CLERESTORY HOUSE WITH UP-HILL PATIO AND ROYER FOYERS. THIS 1,200 SQ. FT. HOUSE WITH AN ADDITIONAL 500 SQ. FT. GREENHOUSE COULD PROBABLY BE BUILT COMMERCIALLY FOR AROUND $10,000; MUCH LESS IF OWNER-BUILT WITH SALVAGED MATERIALS.

If all the beasts were gone, men would die from great loneliness of spirit, for whatever happens to the beast also happens to man.

GABLES

For those who absolutely will not be satisfied unless they have a view directly downhill, who are threatening in their minds to build a First-Thought House despite all we have said, to these people we offer a compromise; the downhill gable.

Gables are peaks which jut out of roofs. They are common sights on above ground houses. Most top floors on peaked roofed houses have gables when that floor is used for habitation rather than as an attic. It can be a way of adding windows and even doors to the downhill side of a Basic Design without creating drainage problems.

We are not overly enthused about gables. Of the Five Methods of Design it is the one we recommend least. Gables jut up out of the Basic Design ruining the purity of form. They are difficult to cover with earth (it tends to slide off). They invite heat loss and are more prone to be buffeted by winds with the corresponding lower wind chill factor. Gables are more conspicuous to neighbors. If a tree falls across a gable it is likely to squash it, whereas if one falls across a Royer Foyer or a normal shed roof there is solid earth in most cases on all sides to absorb much of the blow. Finally, gables present ticklish engineering and construction problems which should not be tackled by the novice. If you are building your first underground house and are not a professional or solid amateur builder, pass up the gable for the time being. The Royer Foyer concept is more for the likes of us.

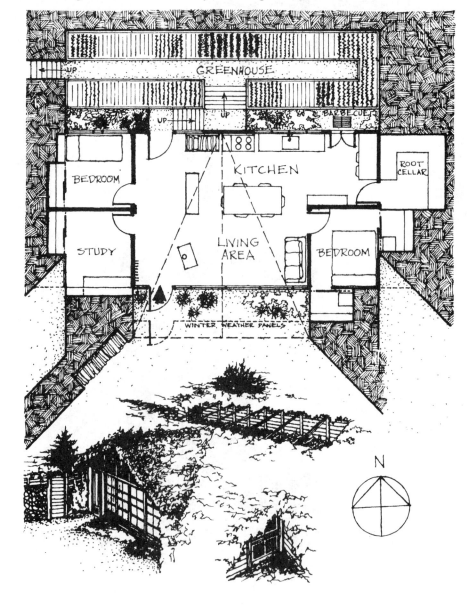

The gabled house depicted here has 700 square feet with an additional 400 square feet of attached greenhouse. It is designed for the limited income homesteader who wishes to do without—or cannot afford—electricity. Kitchen water is provided by catching runoff from the greenhouse covering. Drinking water is hauled. Built commercially, the house should probably sell for under $5,000. Even paying for new carpet, stove and greenhouse roofing, the owner-builder should be able to build for well under half that amount.

Four Eastern Methods of Design

There are four additional methods of getting light and sometimes air and views in an underground. These are favored by the eastern architects, the ones who build with concrete. They are not much used by the owner-builders out west, but in certain instances they may have merit. For this reason we will examine them briefly.

THE FIRST-THOUGHT DESIGN

We have gone into our objections to the First-Thought Design in some detail already. As you recall, the First-Thought involves a house with a facade of windows facing downhill and a solid back wall abutting the hillside. In the worst version of this design the roof is pitched back into the hill backing up the roof runoff against the drainage from the hill. The other common variation has a flat roof. As we have mentioned both of these can cause disastrous drainage problems especially with the PSP system. A French drain will help but in this instance we don't believe it can be relied upon. There is simply too much else going against it.

The First-Thought design does have two advantages: view and possible solar energy adaptation. The view advantages are obvious. The possibilities of solar energy come where the downhill slope is a southern exposure. Whether a person should put this sort of house in an area of high density of housing where it is visible to others is an open question, especially since both views and solar energy may be utilized by more concealed design methods.

If you feel, however, that you absolutely *must* build with this design we have two suggestions: (1) *Put in an Uphill Patio,* and (2) Pitch the roof so that the roof drains off to the sides where the water can run off and downhill away from the house. Unless your soil is exceptionally well drained you will probably want to put in French drains on the side of your house also. Following these suggestions should give you relief from your drainage headaches plus balance of light and cross ventilation.

ATRIUMS

An atrium is a small interior courtyard in a house usually fronted on all sides by windows and sliding glass doors. It is covered in the winter with glass or corrugated plastic greenhouse roofing, or with some other material such as fiberglass. This helps to keep the heat down over the windows and sometimes makes possible a greenhouse.

Our objection to atriums is that the view from any one wall of windows is of three other walls of windows. Aluminum and glass! Compare that to the view of an Uphill Patio with its walls of natural wood terraced and planted with climbing or hanging greenery.

Most atriums seem to be built more with traffic in mind than aesthetic considerations. They function as glass enclosed skylighted hallways. They are an architect's means of handling traffic while bringing light and air into the interior of a First-Thought House. But at what an aesthetic cost. To us they seem little more than a lazy designer's easy way out.

Light and air can and should be brought into the interior, or hillside portion, of a house through the use of the Uphill Patio, Offset Rooms and clerestories. Still, there may be certain instances when an atrium is desirable—if the house were really massive, for example, yet built in a restricted area where the rooms cannot be strung out. How then does one make an atrium attractive?

We offer two suggestions. First, raise the level of the atrium from the floor to chest height. Put windows from that height to the ceiling. This forces the trajectory of view up towards the sky and away from the windows of the other three sides. It makes someone sitting or lying down invisible from the other rooms. Plant the atrium—especially towards the center—with perennial plants which will further block the view of the other windows and doors. This will admittedly cut down somewhat on the amount of light entering the rooms, but the view then will be of an area lush with vegetation, and privacy will be assured. Looking across most atriums from one room to another is much like looking into a goldfish bowl. The result is that people often close off their rooms with ceiling to floor drapes which eliminates both view and light altogether.

All things are connected whatever befalls the earth befalls the sons of the earth.

47

Elevating the atrium would seem to eliminate the hallway or traffic function of the space. People will object to climbing up and down stairs to get to another room ten feet away. Corridors should be dug so that the atrium may be crossed at floor level. The walls of the corridors should probably be of some interesting natural material; logs would be good, or old barn wood, or cedar paneling;

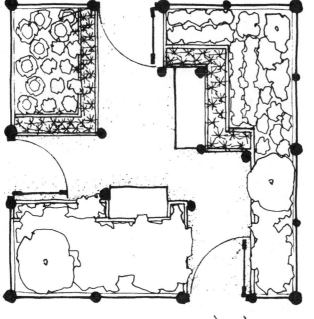

something, anything to give it some character and charm rather than the sterility of concrete, aluminum and glass.

And here is our second suggestion: put a jog, or a bend in the corridors so that the doorway from one room is not visible from another.

Raising the planting beds of the atrium has one additional potential benefit. It raises the growing surface closer to the roof where there is a better chance for the sun to penetrate, especially on winter days when the sun is at a low angle in the sky. With most atriums the sun never reaches the floor except for a few hours during midday in the summer. This makes it so difficult to grow things that most people don't even try. Most of the atriums we've seen are barren of vegetation. The floor is more often than not white gravel with flagstone or concrete walks between the rooms. A few pathetic attempts are sometimes made to liven it up with hanging plants from above and driftwood chunks on the floor but there is no getting around the fact that they are primarily aluminum and glass and concrete or gravel areas. No wonder people pull their drapes.

SKYLIGHTS

Tell anyone that you live in an underground house that has a lot of windows and after the initial puzzlement they suddenly beam, "Oh, you must mean skylights, huh?"

Not a chance. To our way of thinking skylights are more hassle than they are worth. They have these disadvantages:

(1) They bleed the heat out of your house. If a window loses fifteen times more heat than a well insulated wall then a skylight is that much worse for the heat in any given room tends to gather up towards the ceiling.

(2) Skylights often leak, especially when built by non-professionals. If you don't believe this, ask anyone who has built a dome with skylights.

(3) Things tend to fall through skylights. This is not much of a worry on conventional buildings—they, after all, are dozens of feet above ground—but on underground housing, where things often walk over the roof, this can be a real threat. Especially on a homestead. Consider the number of things which could fall through: thrown objects, rolling objects, falling objects, walking or running objects such as goats, cows, horses, bears, children, stone-outs . . . why, the list is endless. If you have been so foolish as to glaze your skylight with regular glass consider what may likely happen if something comes through. The natural tendency is to look towards the source of a sudden sound, which means people below would instinctively look up at the sound of crashing glass—which means those below would get faces and eyes full of showering glass splinters. Now *you*, living in fear of such an eventuality, might duck getting merely a neck and head full of glass, but how about your visitors and children?

If this still does not dissuade you please consider doing these things: (1) cover your skylight with a non-shattering material such as sheets of plastic corrugated greenhouse roofing; (2) double up the sheets so that there is an air space in between for insulation like thermal window panes; (3) raise the skylight a foot or more above your sod roof so that it is both a visual and physical reminder that there is a skylight there, and so that the

drainage from the roof itself is not tempted to congregate around the invisible and all but inevitable gaps in your glazing. If this last suggestion doesn't completely eliminate leaks at least it will reduce considerably the volume of water coming through.

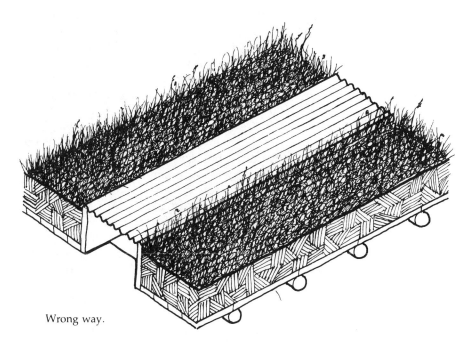

Wrong way.

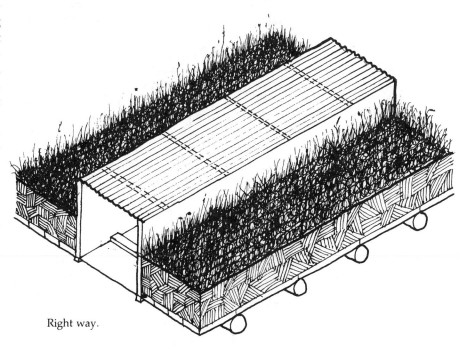

Right way.

LIGHTWELLS

Lightwells are hollow, usually round, shafts of concrete which come from the surface down into the interior of a house to bring in light. The interiors of the shafts are always covered with a reflective paint.

There is no question that lightwells do the job; they can provide a surprising amount of light. They have their place under certain difficult design conditions, particularly where the application is to be an industrial one. Who can deny that, in this era of energy shortage, it is preferable to have a natural light source rather than an artificial one?

However, we do not recommend light shafts for the owner-builder, particularly not for the penny-pinched homesteader. They provide neither view nor (in most cases) ventilation. They solve no drainage problems, can't be used as greenhouses or as barbecue windows.

But the main objection is cost. They are simply prohibitively expensive. In some cases the cost of a ten or fifteen foot concrete light shaft may be more than a homesteader can afford to spend building his entire house. Forget lightwells.

DRAINAGE:

The French Drain

Drainage, we have repeatedly said, is our most worrisome problem with underground housing.

Building at as low a cost as we do with PSP we cannot count on the materials to waterproof the house. Polyethylene, though an absolute moisture barrier, is a frail substance prone to rents and tears. Being amateurs who build these things, our workmanship often leaves something to be desired. That forces us to rely on sound design to pull us through the threat of leaks.

For this reason we will emphasize again and again that you must design so that water never backs up against your house or collects in pockets on the roof. Give water an easy exit and it will take it rather than trying to fight its way through your home's defenses. For this reason the initial consideration on all of our designs is drainage.

We have previously stated how the Basic Design with its shed roof effortlessly dis-

poses of all precipitation falling on top of the house. We have explained how the Uphill Patio intercepts the drainage coming down the hill and gives it a chance to soak into the ground before reaching the house. But what if you are in an area of exceptionally heavy rainfall and/or what if your soils drain poorly? The answer here is the French drain.

The French drain is simplicity itself. It is nothing more than a ditch or trench filled with small rocks or gravel (sand in a real pinch) which gives the water an easy exit away from the house. The bottom of the ditch must be graded for "fall" so that the water runs downhill away from the structure. Water is as reluctant to leave by an uphill route as a journalist is to leave the free bar at a press conference.

If you have any doubts about the soil around your house by all means put in a French drain. Start by putting it the length of the Uphill Patio. Dig a ditch at least a foot below the floor level. Run the ditch around the side of the house which you judge to be the most likely to have drainage problems and off downhill making certain that you have sufficient fall. Should you be in a particularly wet area, you may want to put the drain on all sides of the house from a foot or more below floor level all the way up to roof level. If you happen to be on the Oregon or Washington coast or other area of ridiculous rain, and if your soils are clay besides, you may want to put drain tile at the bottom as an added precaution.

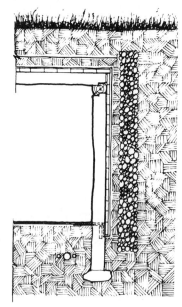

Detail:
French drain.

SPECIAL DESIGNS:

The Ridge House

There is a design site I haven't mentioned yet: the crest of a ridge. Of all possible underground building sites, I guess this has to be my favorite. It is possible to build a U house through the crest of a ridge which will have optimum drainage, spectacular views, and yet be all but invisible to the neighbors below.

I have such a building site on my property in Idaho. It's on a ridge which rises several hundred feet above the valley floor. There is a house under construction there which when completed will offer a view fifteen miles to the south to a mountain called Roman Nose, and thirty-five miles to the north to the Canadian border. Two valleys are visible from the site—Deep Creek and the Kootenay—and two mountain ranges, the Purcells and the Selkirks. My design fully utilizes this panoramic sweep.

Back in 1969 and 1970, before I received the inspiration to go underground, I began a cabin on this ridge. I got the frame up, the floor laid, the roof on, and was beginning to side the thing off when I came to my senses.

I was having a problem with winds there. The winds tore off the roofing. Taking a good look at the trees around the building site I could see that most of them were wind damaged; they had either lost limbs or had snapped completely off at the top. Since the cabin was constructed up on cedar posts with the floor laid on that and the frame built on top of the floor (this is to say it did not have the strength of true pole construction), I began having visions of the whole house blowing off the ridge like a box kite once it was completely sided off. For a while I considered wrapping cables around the roof beams and attaching them to "dead men" (buried logs) to keep the house in place, but it didn't feel right. Eventually I decided to tear the whole mess down and go underground.

The original plan called for one massive room (which could later be partitioned off along the interior support posts). We would cut six feet deep completely through the ridge from one side to the other, shore up the earthen walls and put doors and window glass from floor to ceiling on the two open ends. This is still the basic plan but there are additions.

The open ends face to the north and south. There is a slight fall to the ridge to the west and it is this fall which I planned to utilize to get a pitch to the roof. Since the fall is only two or three feet in the some twenty-four feet which is to be the width of the room it did not seem to be enough pitch to ensure good roof drainage. So...I've decided to raise the eastern portion of the roof some three feet above ground level in a sort of clerestory effect. This should give adequate drainage and at the same time make it possible to add eastern windows to catch the morning sun.

There was still an excellent view to the west which would go unutilized. To the west are the Selkirk mountains. Much of this wall of the house would have to be solid earth to absorb the roof run-off and provide stability of structure. However, there seems to be enough room there to add a gabled kitchen area extended out from the wall which will give the lady of the house the afternoon sun to work by, and the evening sunset. Since kitchens in homestead households are busy areas which must be spacious we'll extend the kitchen into the main room also and partition out the traffic flow by use of a massive built-in dining room table and cabinets and work counters. The end result will be a kitchen which is integrated with the whole house yet is separated by waist-high functional partitions. The kitchen will catch the morning sun, through the clerestory, will have views to the north and south through the walls of windows and will have the single exclusive view to the west. It will be the heart of the house and the lightest, airiest room of all.

Eventual expansion of the house has been taken into consideration. On the southern shoulder of the ridge is an old, grown over logging road. With a minimum of digging this cut can be utilized for rooms stringing off to the east, each of which will have full southern exposure for maximum winter sun. Roof overhang, of course, will provide shade from the high, hot summer sun.

And after defeat, they turn their days in idleness and contaminate their bodies with sweet food and strong drink.

The Ridge House

This is the house the author is most looking forward to building. It is under construction now (has been for several years) high up on his Idaho 40 acres.

The main body of the house cuts through a ridge giving views of fifteen miles to the south and thirty-five miles to the north while remaining all but invisible from other dwellings. This section (kitchen, living room, etc.) is being constructed first. It is designed so that the rooms to the north with their heat bleeding walls of windows may be closed off in the winter to save fuel.

The kitchen (the heart of any true rural household) is placed so that it will be out of the main flow of traffic yet be in sight and

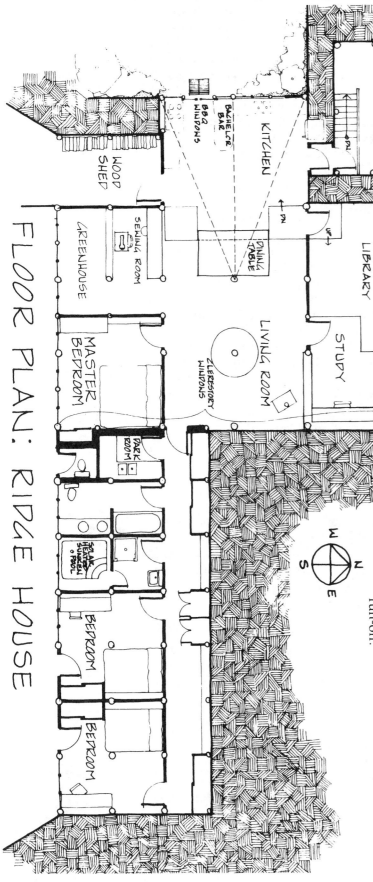

sound of most sections of the house ("What are those kids up to now?"). Though separated only by waist high shelves. People who spend considerable time inside a house appreciate the opportunity to work among greenery.

The sewing and greenhouse areas are rated from the living/dining room area by an elevation change no steps need be climbed up or tripped over when serving at the massive (5'x8') dining room table since this table is incorporated into the level change itself. The table also doubles as a kitchen work table. Depending upon where the worker sits there are possible views in four directions. By sitting on stools on the kitchen side of the table it is possible to look out through the opened doors to the north, or up through the clerestory windows to the north. Sitting on chairs in the dining room section allows views through the sewing and greenhouse areas to the south or out through the gable windows to the west.

The east wing of bedrooms and baths will be built later when time and finances allow. This section features a Japanese-style family bath (solar heated), regular size tub, shower and two toilets. One of the toilets will open to the outside so that those working outdoors need not track up the house.

Unlike the main section which drains to the west, the wing will drain to the north. At a glance this wing would appear to be a First-Thought design, but not so. The potentially disastrous First-Thought design is when a water coming down upon the house. This wing is built into the *crest* where there is not only no drainage coming down the hill, but a steep north drop off to take care of the roof run-off.

FLOOR PLAN: RIDGE HOUSE

52

THE RIDGE HOUSE

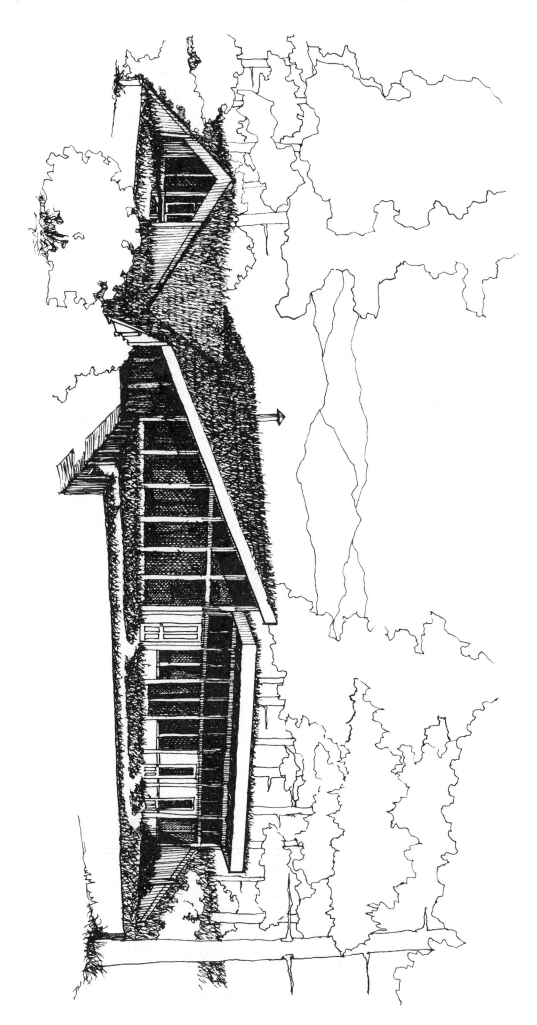

Flat Land Designs

As we have said we aren't much in favor of building on flat land. The land is usually more costly than hilly acreage, there is no warm-southern-slope effect for cold climes nor cool-northern-slope for hot regions. Then flat land is usually prime agricultural land much too much of which is being paved over or built upon in America.

Flat land also presents the designer with two special problems: drainage and view. Obviously, you cannot expect the precipitation landing on the roof to run off down the hill if there is no hill for it to run down. Just as obvious there is not going to be that fine downhill view. However, if flat land is all you have to build in we have designs for you there too.

Consider drainage first. You must make certain that you aren't building in a swampy or marshy area. A test hole dug to several feet below the proposed depth of your house, covered and let stand for some months prior to construction is a fine idea, particularly if you can monitor it frequently during the rainy season or during the spring runoff. This will reassure you that you aren't building below the water table, and give you some idea of the permeability of the soil. (Another way to get an idea of how well your soil will drain is to go to your District Soil Conservation office and request assistance. These federal agents, long ignored by society as a whole, will usually be delighted to help and frequently will come out to your property to give you an on-site appraisal—for free.)

If you discover that your land has a high water table we suggest *strongly* that you do not try to build below that level. There are those who advocate building below water-table and waterproofing the structure, using pumps, etc. We feel that this is just asking for trouble. Our advice is to design several feet above water table even if this means coming above ground and berming earth over the structure. True, you will not technically have an underground house. You will lose much of the root cellar effect, the place will be more subject to weather conditions and it will be

visible to your neighbors, but at least it will still be earth covered and you will not be locking horns with your most troublesome problem, drainage.

In any event, on flat land you will probably want to put in French drains. If you are building in the desert or your soil is sandy or otherwise extremely well drained you can probably eliminate this feature, but in most other cases plan on putting in this sort of drainage.

No land is completely flat. It all drains in some direction or other. Your job is to find that direction. If you have a professional survey crew on your land at any time to, say, find your property boundaries, ask them to find the drainage on your building site, too. It should take them just a few minutes. Otherwise, if you can't get a hold of a transit and do the job yourself, buy a line level, some sturdy nylon string and try to find it by the following method: in the center of your building site rake smooth an area of several square feet to eliminate surface irregularities. Drive a stake there deep enough to withstand the pull of the taut string. Repeat the process driving four more stakes some thirty or forty feet away at the four corners of the compass. Stretch the string between the center stake and one of the four outward stakes and tie it so that the string is as tight as possible. You don't want any sag. Be sure to measure so that the string is exactly the same height from the ground on each stake. Now hang the line level in the *center* of the string and take a reading. By raising the string on the low stake until the bubble reads level you can compute the rate of fall per foot. Check to see that the fall is area wide—not just a local irregularity—by repeating the process up from the highest stake and down from the lowest stake.

Once you've ascertained which way the land falls, design your house so that the rain landing on top of the house flows either (1) directly off a shed roof in the direction of the fall of the land or (2) flows off a peaked or bowed roof to the *sides* and then is led away and down slope by means of a French drain. Obviously you don't want to drain your roof up-slope.

If you are building in an area of high density of housing—the city or subdivision—we suggest you keep your house below surface as much as possible and let your windows and glass doors face out onto sunken patios and greenhouses. This gives you some degree of controlled view just as does the Uphill Patio on the Basic Design for hillsides. Again, we contend that the view of a greenhouse or landscaped sunken patio is far better than the view of the house next door.

If, however, you are building in the country where there are some fine sweeping views you might want to bring your house, or part of it, slightly above ground. This may be done by elevating the shed roof above ground, by gabling, or by the clerestory effect. You will, of course, cover the roof with earth and mulch and encourage vegetation. The vegetation not only looks nice, purifies the air, and encourages wildlife, but it also helps cool the house in the summer by transpiration.

THE ROUND HOUSE

If professional builders are constructing your house and/or if you are building with concrete you might want to try a round house to break out of the box syndrome and have something different. The American Indians being in close harmony with nature believed strongly in round structures—in round just about anything, in fact. It might be difficult to do a round structure by the PSP system but it should be easier with concrete. There is much to be said for the structural integrity of a round concrete house: being curved the walls have the strength of an arch to withstand lateral thrust. Carry the theme further by building round sunken patios which intersect with the curve of the house. I would suggest a pitch to the roof to encourage the drainage to run off even if it is concrete treated with vulcanized waterproofing, though some underground concrete architects seem to have success with flat roofs. To get light and views in the center of the house you could do a clerestory or an elevated garden/greenhouse atrium.

THE BOWED ROOF HOUSE

If you are building a square or rectangularly shaped house you might get good roof drainage and a pleasingly different ceiling effect by bowing the roof. The drainage would run off to the sides where there are French drains and solid earth. The front and back of the house would face out onto sunken patios or greenhouses or both. The roof could come above ground level if you desired the view. The total effect when seen from a distance would be that of a pleasing small landscaped mound or hill.

A few more hours, a few more winters, and none of the children of the great tribes that once lived on this earth,

THE PEAKED ROOF HOUSE

Instead of bowing the roof you might want to put a peak in it like most conventional above ground houses, though the peak need not be so pronounced. The greater the pitch the better the drainage. On the other hand the greater the pitch the harder it is to keep earth up there. It may tend to slide or wash off if the pitch is too great. A steep incline also makes it more difficult to utilize the roof—as a lawn area, for example. The pitch can be minimized somewhat by mounding more earth towards the lower part, though you will always want some surface pitch to encourage surface runoff.

A pitched roof offers the possibility of coming above ground if that is desired. It also offers excellent clerestory and gabling possibilities. Again, the roof should drain into French drains and solid earth while the open ends should face out onto sunken patios and/or greenhouses.

On all of these houses you will want to construct a sufficient roof overhang on the southern exposure to block the high summer sun but little enough to allow the lower angled winter sun to enter. Planting deciduous trees on the south helps there too. The leaves shade the house in the summer while the naked branches allow the winter sun to warm the structure.

56

CLERESTORY FLAT LAND DESIGN

By turning the pitched roofed house into a split level and adding a clerestory, we get the Clerestory Flat Land Design. It is a home with windows and views in four directions. Each room in the house excepting the bathrooms and root cellar (which should be separated farther from the house) has floor to ceiling windows facing either the north or south sunken patios. The living room and master bedroom also have, in addition, windows to the east through the clerestory, and windows to the west through a semi-sunken gable.

Entrance to the lower levels is through the sunken courtyards, the south one of which is a covered greenhouse in the winter. Both the living room and master bedroom have private entrances off outside walkways which also serve as lounging areas either sunny or shaded, whichever one wants to use. Above the work counter in the kitchen is a translucent fiberglass panel which can be opened to allow communication through to the living room (so mother knows what the kids are up to). The master bedroom similarly has a fiberglass panel which may be opened to allow communication down to the kitchen and dining room, or closed for peace and quiet.

A house like this could probably be built commercially for around $15,000.

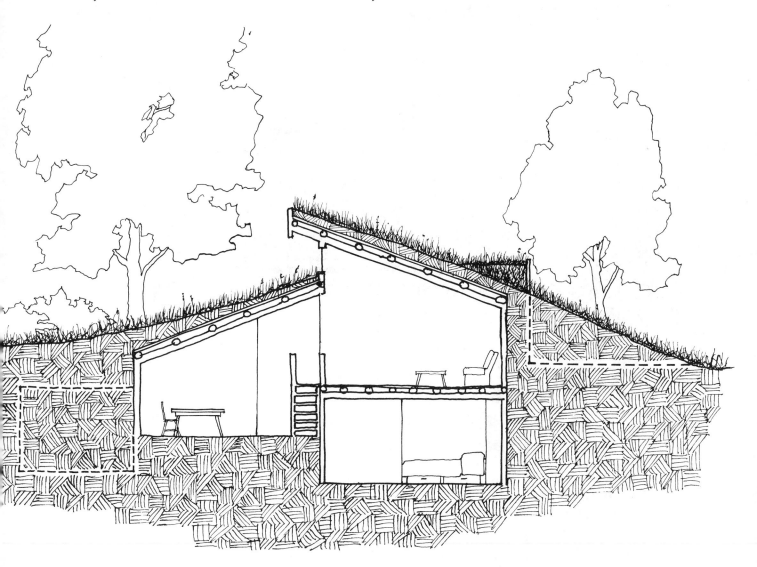

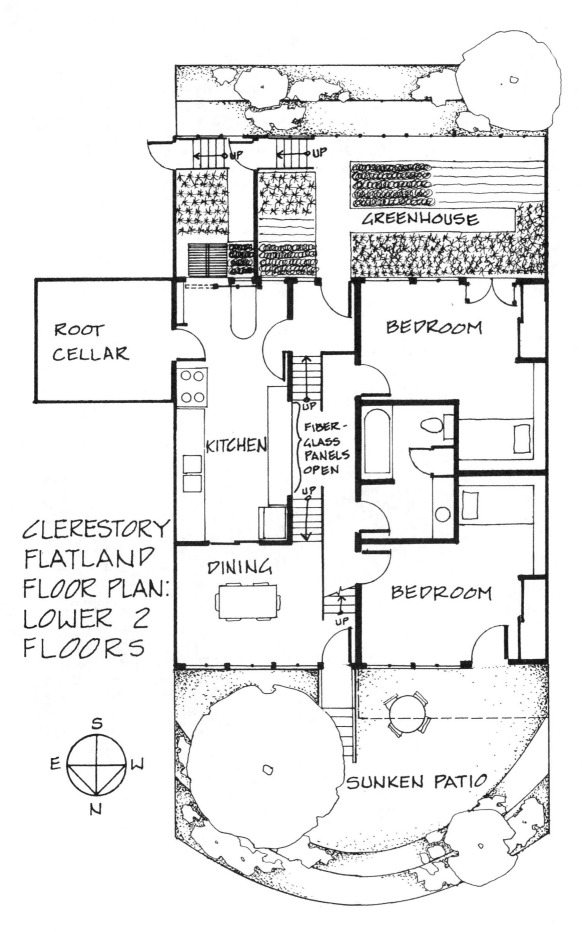

GREENHOUSE

ROOT
CELLAR

BEDROOM

UP

UP

KITCHEN

FIBER-
GLASS
PANELS
OPEN

UP

UP

CLERESTORY
FLATLAND
FLOOR PLAN:
LOWER 2
FLOORS

DINING

UP

BEDROOM

S
E — W
N

SUNKEN PATIO

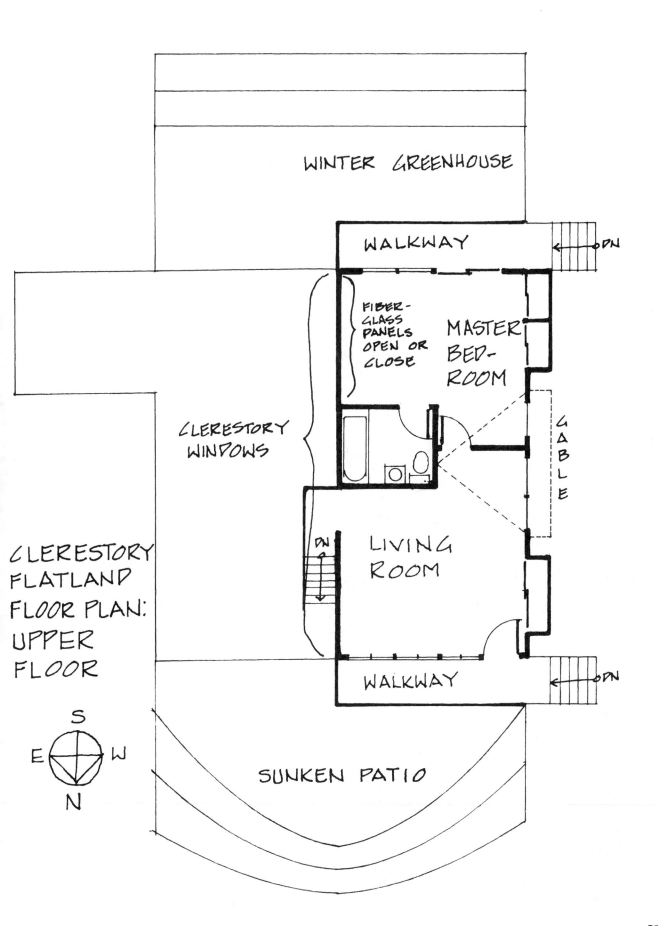

WINTER GREENHOUSE

WALKWAY

DN

FIBER-GLASS PANELS OPEN OR CLOSE

MASTER BED-ROOM

CLERESTORY WINDOWS

GABLE

LIVING ROOM

DN

CLERESTORY FLATLAND FLOOR PLAN: UPPER FLOOR

WALKWAY

DN

S
E W
N

SUNKEN PATIO

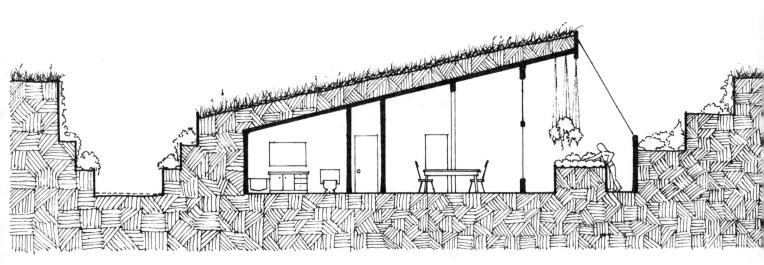

SHED ROOF FLAT LAND HOUSE

Here is another favorite flat land design. This shed roof house has a wall of windows facing south. From the dining and living rooms the windows look out on the greenhouse. From the kitchen the windows face the barbecue area and sunken patio.

The kitchen and living room also have windows which face east and west respectively. These occur where the roof rises above natural ground level. In addition each bedroom has its own set of windows and door facing a sunken landscaped patio. Roof drainage is handled by the sunken patio in the rear of the house which is pitched slightly to encourage any standing water to stand well away from the structure.

A second story could be added above the kitchen and living room by pitching the roof at a steeper angle.

When designing this house the author began by laying out a grid of posts six feet apart. Then he designed within those restrictions. The result was that each post has multiple functions and no post stands alone in the middle of a room.

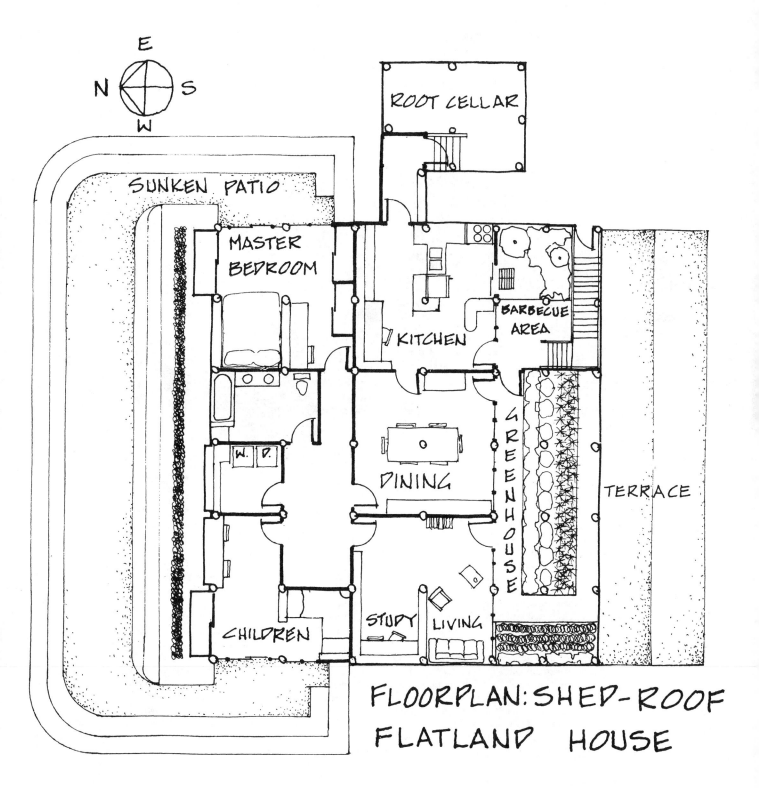

Our God is
the same
God.

E
N S
W

ROOT CELLAR

SUNKEN PATIO

MASTER
BEDROOM

KITCHEN

BARBECUE
AREA

W. D.

DINING

GREENHOUSE

TERRACE

CHILDREN

STUDY   LIVING

FLOORPLAN: SHED-ROOF
FLATLAND HOUSE

61

SUBDIVISIONS

Is there an American with a sense of beauty who doesn't hate the sight of the subdivisions which have defiled our landscape?

Yet here is where underground housing offers one of its greatest potentials. By putting our subdivisions underground we can have neighborhoods of unequaled aesthetic appeal. Walking down the street of an underground subdivision would be like taking a walk in a park, or in the country. The stroller would see beautifully landscaped mounds with only an occasional door or window peeking out.

Subterranean subdivisions would offer the ultimate in privacy and view. It would be possible to design so that no one house would have a view of another. Landscaped mounds of earth separating the sunken patios of the houses would not only ensure visual privacy but would be sound barriers as well.

And there is the added benefit to the home owner of a doubling of his yard space since the roof becomes additional garden or lawn.

These are what subdivisions of the future will be like.

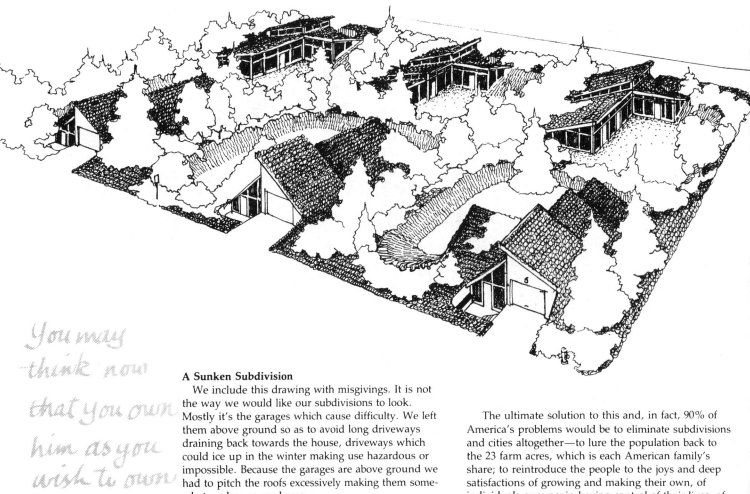

You may think now that you own him as you wish to own our land.

A Sunken Subdivision

We include this drawing with misgivings. It is not the way we would like our subdivisions to look. Mostly it's the garages which cause difficulty. We left them above ground so as to avoid long driveways draining back towards the house, driveways which could ice up in the winter making use hazardous or impossible. Because the garages are above ground we had to pitch the roofs excessively making them somewhat useless as yard area.

In certain areas these technical difficulties may be overcome and the garages buried. For example, drainage problems could be reduced considerably—soil conditions allowing—with the use of precast porous concrete blocks in place of slab driveway pavement. A better idea would be to group the garages on a community basis. Better yet would be to design communities where private automobiles are unnecessary.

The ultimate solution to this and, in fact, 90% of America's problems would be to eliminate subdivisions and cities altogether—to lure the population back to the 23 farm acres, which is each American family's share; to reintroduce the people to the joys and deep satisfactions of growing and making their own, of individuals once again having control of their lives, of living in harmony with the natural order.

Though getting closer, America is still not quite ready for this. So we present this subdivision, above ground garages and all, as an interim step, as something the average American can relate to. If we can just get the nation to earth-over her buildings we will have taken the first big leap back to sanity. Then we can begin the rebuilding of society in earnest. . . .

62

SPECIAL EFFECTS

Windows When There Is a Restricted Patio Area

If you want to put windows into a place where there is no possibility of having a proper sunken patio—right on the edge of your property line, for example—you should probably consider using frosted glass or stained glass windows.

Nothing looks worse than those awful window wells which are so common a sight out of basement windows. Usually constructed of drab, grey concrete they extend out only a foot or so and always seem to be cluttered with leaves, mud, paper debris and the like. Unfortunately, this is the mental image many people conjure up when they try to envision windows in an underground house. It is a mental image which perhaps more than any other has hindered the advancement of underground architecture.

Frosted or stained glass can do much to remedy this situation. So can sinking the window well lower. No sense in having just one foot of window up towards the ceiling if you can have a pleasant translucent or stained glass pattern halfway down enlivening what otherwise might be a dark dreary wall. Reflective paint on the window well surface will help throw considerably more light in than will just concrete or bare wooden shoring.

For those with limited means "clear" or frosted fiberglass is recommended. The clear fiberglass is our favorite. Not really clear at all, it will disguise the sight of the well while refracting sunlight in a manner which is really pleasant to view.

In the winter you can cover the window well on the outside with the fiberglass. You'll still get light while keeping in the heat.

Mirrors

One of the devices which have the greatest potential for adding to the livability of underground houses, and which is least used, are mirrors. They are so little used, in fact, that I have heard of only one instance—in New York—in which they have been employed to date.

Frequently on warm, sunny afternoons when I have the glass door to my Royer Foyer open and latched against the outside retaining wall the sunlight is reflected in. This always reminds me of the potential of mirrors and makes me wish I had some hung out there.

Think of the possibilities. Mirrors hung on the shoring of a north side Uphill Patio could beam sunlight into an underground home; a way of getting sunlight through north windows. At other times the sunlight might be beamed down onto the plants of the patio greenhouse doubling the growing rays to plants on winter days. Or consider the view potential. If the mirrors were large enough and pitched at the right angle it could be a way of getting a view downhill over the roof while looking uphill. The same thing could be true of mirrors placed on the shoring of a Royer Foyer; it could help both to beam sunlight into a home during hours when it would not otherwise enter, and could give the occupants views from angles not readily obtainable.

If the wall of windows on an Offset Room face west catching the afternoon sun, mirrors against the opposing patio retaining wall could beam morning sunlight through as well. The reverse is true for offset windows facing east.

The mirrors should probably be hung on hinges with latches on the opposite side so that they may be adjusted to different angles at various times of the day for different effects. Those hung on the shoring of Uphill Patios might best be hinged at the bottom to allow sunlight to enter the house, to beam the rays down onto the plants, or to provide the downhill view. Those hung on the shoring of Royer Foyers would likely be most effective when hinged on the side closest to the windows of the house.

The trouble is mirrors are expensive. They are good items for homesteaders to watch for at auctions, flea markets, second hand shops and the like. There is also the possibility of making purely reflective mirrors by spraying the backs of salvaged windows with reflective paint. This would not probably provide much in the way of view, but it should do a fine job of reflecting the sun, judging from the excellent job my glass door alone does.

But you cannot.

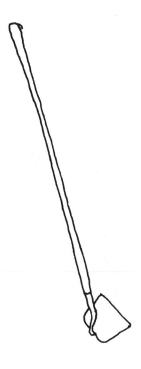

Air Scoops

Air scoops are like those big funnels you see on old steamships. The function of an air scoop is to catch the breeze and send it down under pressure to the area needing ventilation.

I know very little about air scoops. The only time I ever saw one in operation was on a passenger ship. It might not even have occurred to me to consider them in conjunction with underground housing had not a lady mentioned them in an early issue of *Alternative Sources of Energy Magazine* in an article about an underground house she planned to build.

The idea fails to excite me. I can see its application under certain conditions; where the house to be built is massive with many interior rooms and is jammed into a lot too small to allow the stringing out of the structure with a number of sunken patios; or, where they are to ventilate rooms beneath rooms; or under certain industrial conditions.

But for the homesteader/builder they are an unnecessary and expensive frill. Built properly with the five approved methods of design a house gets plenty of cross ventilation. The house to be built by the lady was to be a First-Thought house. She had to do something to get cross ventilation in there. We hold that windows are better.

SPECIAL FEATURES

Building underground gives you the opportunity to add special features to your house which are impractical on surface structures. They are some of the many pluses of underground construction and part of why building below is so exciting. As you build, or after you have lived down under for a while, you might invent some of your own to add to the list.

Barbecue Windows

Perhaps no feature of my house has caused as much comment from visitors, proven more practical, or provided as much satisfaction as the barbecue windows.

These windows, which open in, face out on a portion of the Uphill Patio which is waist high. The patio at this point is very confined. It's more like a window well than a true Uphill Patio. (This is due to the fact that I wanted to save two trees growing above, but no matter.) Because it is so confined there is considerable protection from the wind—an important factor as we shall see. This confinement also seems to create something of a draft, or chimney effect.

Sometime in the first several months after moving into the $50 underground house, I decided to try a cooking fire out there. This was due to the draft and smoke problems I was having with the fire window where I had been cooking. I dug a small pit in the earth, put some bricks around the edge of the pit and used a salvaged steel oven rack for a cooking grate. It was now possible to cook outdoors just by reaching through the windows.

The advantages to this feature are numerous. It allows you to cook outdoors while standing inside out of the rain, hot sun or other weather conditions. It allows you to cook outside while remaining inside convenient to your kitchen—you don't have to carry everything out. It allows you to cook at a comfortable waist high level, not hunkered down over a campfire. It allows you to barbecue from the inside over charcoal or local wood without installing costly, trouble prone, energy consuming fire hoods or other smoke eliminating devices. Because you are actually cooking outside, the fire does not heat up your cool underground home on hot days. In the evening, or at night, the fire throws a fine mellow flickering glow up onto the ceiling, rafters and on some of the walls of the house.

In the winter when it is too cold to open the windows for extended periods, you will cook on your kitchen or heating stove. The barbecue area then becomes an accessible wood storage area, as convenient as opening your windows. As much as a week's supply of firewood may be stored out there at one time ending both unpleasant trips out into the cold and the mess of sawdust, wood chips and bark which always litter the floor when wood is stored in the house.

The warm weather system is not foolproof. If you cook with wet or rotten wood, and if there are strong wind gusts that day, and if there are other windows or doors open in the house creating an interior draft, the smoke may be sucked inside. This can be alleviated to some degree by shutting the windows when you're not actually stirring the pots or turning the food.

But what if you are rushed and must cook with wood that has been out in the rain, and you have a house full of visitors who keep coming in and out continually opening the main door which creates an interior draft due to that day's high wind gusts, and the house begins to fill with smoke and some well meaning soul opens an upper level window to let the smoke draw out but which serves only to draw more in, and everyone is beginning to cough and gasp and throw you watery-eyed looks which clearly doubt your sanity and reason and imply that they think *very little* of you and all of the bragging you have done about the wonders of your damnable barbecue windows—what then?

Well then, friends, you close the barbecue windows, go through the patio door shutting it firmly behind you and—smugly—resume cooking from your new position in:

The Patio Barbecue Area

You may still choke and gasp from the smoke—that's not going to change until you get some dry wood or until those strong gusts die down—but at least your critics can now open some doors and windows and breathe again.

The patio barbecue area will allow you to cook outside in nice weather, to actually *be* outside, not just leaning through a window. Few things can activate this writer's male chauvinistic tendencies—indeed cause him to snarl with contempt—as much as hearing some vacant-headed woman accost her man with the question, "How would *you* like to stay inside cooking over a hot stove on a nice day like this?" I wouldn't like to, and so I don't. I do what women always did before they lost every single last shred of intelligence: I cook outside.

In the warm, predictably good weather months of July and August I often move the whole kitchen outside on the lower terrace

near the Royer Foyer. In addition, I usually set up a second kitchen, a field-kitchen, complete with cooking pots, pans and utensils, plates and food supply at the site of whatever big project is going at the moment. There I cook over a camp fire.

But in the spring and fall months when the weather, though often nice, is unpredictable I use the patio barbecue area. This allows me the luxury of cooking outside with a minimum of fuss. There is little fuss because the outside area is close to the kitchen and all the materials and utensils needed may be passed outside through the barbecue windows in just a few moments. In case of rain they may be passed back in again just as quickly, and the cooking process continued through the windows over the same fire. The cooking is rarely, if ever, interrupted.

The patio barbecue area is a way of making optimum use of the lowest part of the Uphill Patio. Little in the way of vegetation grows there since the sun rarely hits, but this lack of sun is an advantage to the cook; it's not always pleasant to be working over a hot fire when the sun is hot on you too.

Make this part of the patio roomy enough to put a table and bench or stools there and you can serve and eat outside with the same minimum amount of fuss. Carry through the same decor of the room adjacent to the patio— if the paneling in the house is painted white, paint the patio shoring white; if it is unpainted inside, leave it natural outside; if you have indoor/outdoor carpeting inside, lay a piece of it on the ground outside—and you will create a wonderfully livable and functional outdoor extension of your house.

The Bachelor Bar

There is one other special feature related to the barbecue windows which must be mentioned; the Bachelor Bar. This feature has not been built yet, to my knowledge. That I haven't built one yet for myself is solely due to the fact that there is not enough space in my house, though I have wished a thousand times that there were. You may bet that all of my future houses will include this feature.

The Bachelor Bar is a work/eating counter which is built perpendicular to, and just to one side of, the barbecue windows. It should be high enough to make cooking preparations

And his compassion is equal for the redman and the white.

65

on it comfortable from a standing position for whoever is likely to do most of the cooking in your household. This will raise it a little above the height of the average kitchen table.

The Bachelor Bar makes it possible to prepare food on one surface (the bar) while cooking on another (out the windows in the barbecue pit) without taking a step. All you have to do is swivel on your heels to work one area or the other. It further makes it possible to *sit* while doing these things. The slight additional height will require a stool for this.

It has the additional advantage of allowing you to eat while sitting and continuing the cooking process at the same time. One hot course after another can come off the fire without you getting up once. This bachelor is tired of jumping up from the table to stir a pot or flip a hotcake during a meal, hence the name.

If you are serving others you can put them on stools across the bar and cook, serve them, and eat your own meal without ever getting up. This way you will never have to field the annoying question, "When are you going to sit down and eat?" This way, too, your guests or family will never be put in the position of feeling guilty.

A Bachelor Bar

Built-in Greenhouses

In another section we have gone into the possibilities of constructing a greenhouse from the Uphill Patio. We mentioned how the heat radiation from the earth supplements the trapped and stored solar energy and combines with the heat loss from the windows of the house to automatically heat the greenhouse under most conditions without an additional heat source. It's been pointed out that this will in fact save the owner fuel for it keeps the heat down over the windows like storm windows. Here are some additional things to consider:

The shoring for the terraces, if constructed from rock, will retain the solar energy of the day and radiate it back into the greenhouse far longer during the night than will wooden retaining walls. The possible disadvantage here is that the rocks, each being separate entities glued together with concrete, may in time push in with the thrust from the hillside. I have difficulty seeing how a rock wall can be reinforced and integrated into the frame structure of the house downhill as can be done easily with a PSP retaining wall.

The corrugated greenhouse plastic or fiberglass covering makes a fine water collector. This water may be stored and used in the kitchen or bathroom or as irrigation for the plants in the greenhouse. If you have no water supply this could be vital to your comfort and well being. Even if you do have a water source, the fact that the covering keeps surplus water out of the Uphill Patio could be a deciding factor in the livability of your house in such wet areas as the Pacific Northwest rain forests. In those areas if you have no use for the water you will probably want to catch the runoff and divert it away from the roof to keep the soil there from washing down.

In really cold climates, a nighttime insulator covering may be made from old tent canvas, old parachutes, old blankets or any other material you can scrounge up. These should probably be quilted with straw, cloth bits, cattail heads or similar material forming the stuffing. Spread these quilts over the greenhouse in the evening, secure them, and in the morning fold them up and put them away somewhere. You will probably need to construct catwalks between the plastic or fiberglass sheets to facilitate the spreading of the covers. You may want the catwalks anyway to be able to get up there to sweep snow off.

In cold climates when there is little winter sun, your plants will probably stop growing at some point if you are not able to use artificial grow lights. This is unfortunate, but not a knockout punch. It is possible to keep many plants alive and healthy even if in a relatively dormant state of growth. It will still be possible for you to harvest and enjoy them. You just have to be careful of your planting schedule, timing the plants so that they reach maturity or near to maturity before the sun wanes. Only the experience of trial and error will tell you what and when to plant. You should also coordinate the growth of your greenhouse with the growth and harvest of your outdoor garden.

In 1977, with the help of a high schooler named Dave Eskin, I built an experimental solar/geothermal greenhouse on some flat land to the north of a high ridge. There is a gap in the ridge so we positioned the greenhouse to make full use of the three hours of sunlight which came through the gap in November. During the other hours of those November days the ridge blocked the sun. Yet my plants lived on with no supplemental heat or light source. I didn't lose the delicate ones, the tomatoes, cucumbers and beans until late November—seven weeks after the first killing frost. Early in December we had a real three day cold snap; the days were 15 degrees and the nights went as low as zero. I checked my remaining plants during the cold snap and found them frosted over and drooping. That looked like the end of the greenhouse plants that year.

But on a whim I checked the greenhouse again on the ninth of December and found, to my amazement, cabbage, radishes, parsley and lettuce still alive and edible. There were some freeze spots but they were easily trimmed out. So this solar/geothermal greenhouse turned out to be a roaring success. At the very least it will double my growing

season, for I can plant in the greenhouse several months early also. (I write this in the winter of 1977-78 so I haven't been able to complete the experiment yet.)

It is important to remember that this greenhouse did not have many of the benefits of an Uphill Patio greenhouse. First of all, since it was built on the flats, it was necessary to elevate the north side of it to make an optimum angle of sun penetration through the fiberglass. Though we bermed earth back of the north wall it was still not getting the full benefits of the geothermal heat. Besides, raising it exposed it to the wind. On a southern slope your greenhouse can and should be flush with the ground.

The greenhouse was getting only a portion of each day's sun. Your Uphill Patio greenhouses should do much better. When choosing your building site remember that the sun sinks much lower in the winter than in the summer. If you build in a ravine a ridge to the south could block the sun.

There was no nighttime insulation over the greenhouse. Some snow after the cold snap undoubtedly helped there, however.

Perhaps the most important advantage that this greenhouse lacked, though, was the heat loss from the house windows with which your greenhouse will be blessed. It's a free source of supplemental heat.

One unusual advantage that the greenhouse did have was a cold-sink or geothermal radiator. But that explanation is for another day. The point here is that attached and/or sunken greenhouses work.

We have been promoting greenhouses built into the Uphill Patio. We expect them to be practical also when built over Royer Foyers and gables except when these face north. They will help to keep the heat down over the windows and doors though you may probably expect the plants to freeze out eventually due to more glazed surface and less earthen area to radiate heat. Then, too, these are usually entrances and the plants will be subject to cold blasts of air when the outside door is opened. All the more reason for constructing them, however. They will keep those cold blasts from entering the house. If nothing else these greenhouses should be fine areas for starting plants early in the spring.

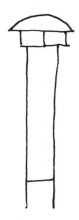

Even the clerestories offer mini-greenhouse possibilities. Extend the roofs out several feet and construct some hinged, sliding or removable windows for the outside. These windows may be glass since they will be vertical rather than horizontal and nothing is likely to come crashing through them as might happen with a skylight surface. Window glass will also allow a view—a big attraction with clerestories. You should have a second set of windows on the inside which you can open to allow you to work on the plants and to provide ventilation in the warmer months. Plant in the enriched soil of the roof.

You may do well to add rabbit cages and worm tanks and possibly even fish tanks to your greenhouses. The rabbits will consume the surplus of oxygen generated by the plants and convert it back to carbon dioxide thus solving a problem which plagues the owners of many sealed greenhouses. Rabbits provide a small amount of body heat to the greenhouse though this factor may be insignificant. The meat they provide won't be insignificant, however. It is highest in protein of all the domestic animals. Rabbits have the best conversion rate of food to meat. Cattle require 20 pounds of feed to produce a pound of beef. Hogs require 9 (I think) pounds of food to provide one pound of pork. Chickens are four to one. But rabbits—glory be—are three to one. Rabbits may be sold or eaten. Their pelts make fine clothing. Rabbits are excellent neighbors. They do not stomp around in the morning shouting cock-a-doodle-do. They don't even say moo when you are late for the milking.

If your greenhouse is large enough and your rabbits are few enough you may be able to feed them from the waste and surplus from your vegetable beds. What food falls through the cages, and the manure that goes with it, make the ideal combination of food for worms so you will want worm tanks below. The worms deodorize the manure quickly and turn it into potting soil for which commercial greenhouses pay good money. Or you may wish to use the soil yourself. The worms can be sold to fishermen or added to your garden or thrown to the chickens or fed to the fish if you have greenhouse fish tanks. The fish may be sold, or they may be eaten. The innards of the fish, when buried in the

Underground Structures
Built with Mike Oehler's (Dirt Cheap) Building Method

Light, air and views emphasized.

Post/shoring/polyethylene method proven since 1971.

To the left: Mike Oehler's original $50 underground house as viewed from the $500 addition. HGTV frequently features this house on its special, "The Subterraneans."

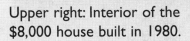

Upper right: Interior of the $8,000 house built in 1980.

Center right: Exterior of the $8,000 house. This house is entirely earthen sheltered except for door and window areas.

Lower right: This interior photo of the $8,000 underground house was photographed with natural light.

The $8,000 house was designed and half built by Mike Oehler. The client built the other half. Mike no longer builds for clients, though he still occasionally consults or designs.

All prices mentioned are from the 1970s and 1980s.

MOLE PUBLISHING CO., PO BOX 6003 MISSOULA, MT 59806 • 800 328-8790
WWW.UNDERGROUNDHOUSING.COM

Above: A six-room underground home built in 1981 for $2000. The owner/builder was a sawmill-owning logger who worked up his own lumber.

Right: Some of the windows in an eight-bedroom, 5,000-square-foot underground house and greenhouse built in Idaho in the early 1980s for $20,000. Had it been built above ground at the then national building average of $50 per square foot it would have cost the family $250,000. This family saved $230,000.

Left: An underground house built by Mike Oehler's methods in Holland.
Below: Mike emerges from his hillside Earth Sheltered Greenhouse, a P/S/P structure that has been in service since 1979.

Mike is currently building the Ridge House (not pictured here.) He expects the final cost of this 4-bedroom, 2-bath, 1800 sq ft solar home will be under $30,000. Though underground, it will have views of up to 30 miles.

soil, make excellent fertilizer. So does the water from the fish tanks when you change it while irrigating your greenhouse plants (both at once). The fresh water for the fish comes from the runoff from the greenhouse covering.

All of which is to say your greenhouse can go a long way to support you. It can also purify the air for your house, no small advantage in this era of air pollution. It can provide you with organically grown and raised foods the quality of which you are certain.

Root Cellar/Fallout Shelter/ Wine Cellar

One of the special features which you should include is a root cellar. If you are a back-to-the-lander this is a must.

Since, as a homesteader, you are going to need one anyway, why not build it as an extension of your house? An underground house offers the perfect opportunity. You can end those freezing walks in the winter, end shoveling snow drifts away from the root cellar door, end the possibility of your food ever freezing, end the possibility of theft or pilferage, and even be able to exercise a close degree of varmint control. Built into the wall right next to your kitchen, and incorporated with the Uphill Patio/greenhouse concept, you will have the enviable luxury of perhaps your whole winter food supply, both fresh and stored, just a few steps from your kitchen table. Safeway can't offer you that.

We aren't going to go into the benefits of a root cellar here. Everyone who knows the first thing about homesteading knows that they are a necessity, as important to a homestead as a water supply or as a garden area. Instead we are going to make a few practical suggestions.

In most climatic zones the root cellar should be built into solid earth off to the side of, and a few steps down from, the kitchen. The warmer the climate the lower the cellar should be. This is to allow more of the earth's cooling capacity to go to work during the warm months and to allow the cool air to stay there when the door is opened. In areas of permafrost—solidly frozen earth—such as interior Alaska and northern Canada we suggest keeping the root cellar at nearly the same level as the kitchen floor. This will allow some of the coldest air to escape and to be supplanted by warmer air when the door is opened. If this raises the root cellar too close to the surface just pile more earth on top during construction. In all cases, the wall between the kitchen and the root cellar should be solidly insulated.

Since a root cellar is by definition a windowless room with three or more feet of earth on the roof you might want to design with the possibility of having it do double duty as a fallout shelter.

We are aware that the majority of our readers will scoff at the idea of having a fallout shelter. The idea of a nuclear war is unthinkable to most Americans, which is an interesting bit of national schizophrenia considering the fact that America has spent hundreds of billions of dollars to make her participation in a nuclear war effective. The Russians do not scoff at the idea. It is, in fact, Soviet national policy to construct fallout shelters. So is it with China. The Chinese have been digging like crazy for years and all of their cities are undermined with fallout shelters. Chinese leaders have repeatedly stated that they *expect* nuclear war. The same conclusion was reached by a task force of Harvard professors who studied the question. As reported in *Time Magazine*, the professors stated that since Westinghouse and General Electric have been actively promoting and marketing nuclear power plants around the world, and since the waste products of nuclear power plants are easily converted into atomic weaponry, atomic bombs are going to be as common among nations by the end of the century as are "Saturday Night Specials" in American cities today. The professors concluded that atomic war happening somewhere on this planet by the year 2000 is not a possibility, but a probability.

You may not care if you live after a nuclear war, but how about your family?

It takes little extra effort to adapt a root cellar to use as a fallout shelter. There should probably be a wall of earth between the main body of the house and the shelter/root cellar. There should be a passageway leading to the shelter with doors at either end which can be sealed tight. (The passageway can be built

Continue to contaminate your bed, and you will one night suffocate in your own waste.

with shelves and used for storage.) Having a supply of empty sandbags or even burlap bags (obtainable from many feed stores) which can be filled with dirt from the floor of the shelter in time of crisis and stacked against the door would be a good idea. The civil defense people can tell you how to set up an air filtering system. The system could draw from the main part of the house where the air would contain less radioactive dust. Food storage shelves in the root cellar could be constructed wide enough and high enough apart so that your family could sleep on them. In normal times they could hold food stuffs which could be cleared off. Sealable plastic bags could handle the body waste problem. All that remains then is the lighting system, radio, water supply and other items which the Civil Defense can also advise you on.

While you are at it you could build wine racks to hold either the store bought kind or your own homemade product. As a wine cellar the room would have a triple function. That way there would be at least some cheer during the weeks of waiting through the fallout.

Built-in Closets and Shelves

Another fine advantage to underground housing is that you may build closets and shelves into any wall which is solid earth. You can't do this on an above ground structure; there would be lumps and protrusions all over the outside of the house. On underground housing these go unnoticed.

The only requirement here is that the walls of the closets and shelves be integrated with

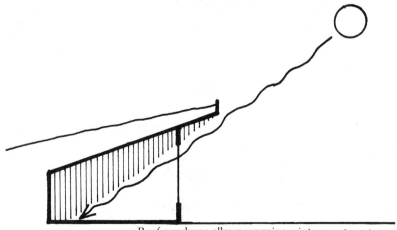

Roof overhang allows warming winter sun to enter house . . .

the structural members—the posts—of the house. They must be able to withstand pressure. As explained in the section on construction, the pressure of the earth on one wall is transferred across the house and counterbalanced by the pressure exerted against the opposite wall. The closet and shelves built behind the posts must be able to withstand this. Aside from that there is no limit to the number you may build, or to the depth you may build them. You can run wild with this concept and perhaps for the first time in your life have enough closet space.

Built-in Coolers

It is quite possible to have refrigeration without mechanical means whatsoever, without the use of electricity, kerosene or gas. There are two types of passive coolers: air cooled and earth cooled. By utilizing a combination of the two most of your daily needs will be met nicely.

My *air cooler* was built into the $50 house from the beginning. A neighbor gave me an old stand-up glass doored cabinet which I positioned so that it became a part of the wall on the Uphill Patio. The cabinet has two sets of doors. The upper ones are the glass ones, while the lower set are wooden. Since the patio is waist high at this particular section, I reinforced the back of the lower part of the cooler so that it functions as shoring holding back the earth of the patio. On the shelves in the lower part I store potatoes, onions, apples and the like. These are refrigerated to a mild degree by the earth which is on two sides (the cooler is in the corner of the house.)

The upper portion of the cooler, the part serviced by the glass doors, has no earth behind it. So I removed the back and replaced it with window screen. In the summer time this allows air circulation. At night the foods are always cool enough. Even during the day they are considerably cooler than the surrounding surface temperatures. This is because the cool air hangs down in the lower portion of that north patio where the sun rarely hits. The cooler also benefits on these days from the cool of the house. Even on 90 degree days the foods won't much warm above 70 degrees. Sometimes on those days I place damp rags over the foods. If someone really wanted to get into it they could rig up a system which drips water over the rags, but I have never found this necessary.

During the cold months I thumbtack clear polyethylene over the window screen. This keeps the food from freezing. The items which need the most refrigeration I put closest to the polyethylene on the lowest shelves.

The combination of window screen/polyethylene/glass doors allows light to enter the house through the cooler brightening up what could otherwise be a gloomy corner. Thus the cooler serves a triple function: it's a cooler, it's part of the wall of the house and it's a light source. I count the glass doors as two of the windows on the house.

I continually marvel that so few other people have utilized this system. I have, in fact, seen only one other system which is remotely close to this. It is at that most interesting of all high schools, Pacific School, just south of San Francisco in the Santa Cruz mountains. There the environmentally aware kids have constructed and use a refrigerator which juts out of a wall on the side of their kitchen. The foods are naturally refrigerated at night and during the winter by the cool coastal breezes. During the day there is an electrical refrigerating system which kicks on just as with any other refrigerator. A conservative estimate is that they save 30% of the

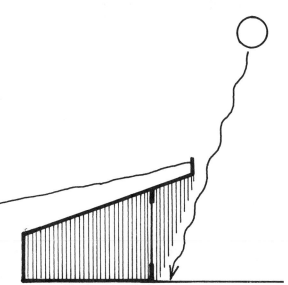

but blocks hot summer sun.

energy needed to cool their considerable food supply. I doubt whether the foods at M.I.T. and Cal Tech are kept in systems which are 30% energy efficient.

An *earth cooler* is particularly suited to underground housing. An earth cooler is no more difficult to build than digging a hole in your floor and lining it, putting on a cover and throwing some insulation over it. The insulation may be as simple as an old blanket, or, if you are a slob, your winter coat.

Remember first of all that your house, being underground, will rarely register temperatures above 70 or 75 degrees even on the hottest days (assuming that you keep the windows and doors closed during the heat—you open them at night). Now consider the fact that a few feet down the earth temperature is likely to be around 55 degrees, and you have the secret of the system. The cool air, being heavier, will hang in at the bottom of the cooler. I used to have a garbage can sunk into the floor of my house. Sometimes on hot days when I had visitors I would amuse myself by handing the guests a jar of mayonnaise just pulled from the bottom of the garbage can. As soon as they felt the coldness of the jar I'd be rewarded with a look of astonishment.

During the hottest months an earth cooler will keep a jug of unpasteurized cow's milk fresh for four days, especially if you put a damp rag over it. You will surely want an everyday earth cooler in your kitchen area somewhere. The closer to a north wall and the further from the stove the better. For additional, even colder, refrigeration, sink a roomy cooler in the floor of your root cellar.

Firewindows

Firewindows are windows added to the lower corner of a room which, for whatever reason, is only three or four feet from floor to ceiling.

The firewindow on my $50 underground house gets its name because originally I had cooking and camp fires out there at night. It was pleasant to lie in bed comfortably snug in the house and stare into a camp fire. Comfortable, that is, until the smoke began to draw up through the house, as it usually seemed to do. Maybe it was the shed roof which drew it up, I don't know, but it was a nuisance. It forced me to keep the window closed which wasn't nearly so much fun.

Not that I regret having the window. Nothing of the sort. It was a blessing. It gave me an emergency exit, reading light when I sat in bed, and cross ventilation. It gave me a view down the ravine. Kids love to climb in and out of it. As a gag, I still occasionally lead first time visitors through it into the house on their hands and knees, telling them that it is the main entrance. The firewindow was the

inspiration for the later invented Royer Foyer.

I still haven't given up on it as a firewindow. One of these years when I'm rich and idle I'm going to weld together a portable fireplace from some light metal, maybe sheet metal. I'll add a portable chimney and, presto, I'll have an instant fireplace for rainy days and winter months. On good days, I'll take it away and have a window again.

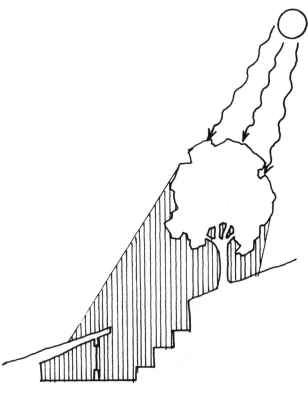

Deciduous trees allow warm winter sun to enter while blocking hot summer sun.

Chapter 6
MATERIALS; WHERE TO BUY AND SCROUNGE

There are a number of secrets to keeping the cost down on your own house. Among them are:

(1) building small and adding on later as time and finances allow;
(2) avoiding the building codes;
(3) doing without such amenities as plumbing and electricity;
(4) doing the labor yourself or with friends;
(5) gathering cheap or free material, or working it up yourself; and, of course,
(6) building underground with the PSP system. This item alone gives you a roaring advantage over conventional surface builders; half of your material is right on the site and is absolutely free. Mother Earth is hard to beat for economy.

With the exception of the joy of building there are few parts of the project as much fun as scrounging material. It's exhilarating. It's like being the first one in a bargain basement at the start of a sale. It's like finding a hundred dollar bill on the ground. When you make a big score it's as though you just won a lottery.

Wrecking Buildings

By far your best chance of landing a windfall of free material is to tear down someone's old building. You may have to agree to turn over some of the salvaged material to the owner or you may get to keep it all yourself depending on what sort of deal you strike. Be choosy. There are a lot more buildings to be torn down than you may think at first, at least out West there are. Sometimes owners have to advertise for weeks to get someone to agree to do the job.

An old house is a gold mine. You can get windows, plumbing fixtures, pipes, insulation (maybe), structural members, nails, siding, and some fine old tongue-in-groove flooring. Sometimes you can get bricks or cinder blocks. Air ducts or radiators are another possibility. If you salvage carefully you may get most of the materials needed to build a new house.

Old barns and sheds are rewarding also. You won't get as much variety of material but you'll get some fine lumber. You may get the real stuff, not the ¾" and 1½" which is sold for 1" and 2" lumber today. One difficulty

and the view of the ripe hills blotted by talking wives,

DEMOLITION AGREEMENT

This agreement executed by and between the Property Owner, below named and the Wrecker-Salvager, below named, provides as follows:

RECITALS

1. Property Owner: _____

2. Wrecker-Salvager: _____

3. Location of Property:_____

_____

4. Description of Structure: _____

_____

5. Consideration: Amount:_____, paid by _____

   to:_____

6. Length of Time to be completed: _____

NOW THEREFORE IT IS MUTUALLY AGREED AS FOLLOWS:

1. That Property Owner shall permit the demolition of the structure described above on the property described above and Wrecker-Salvager agrees to demolish the same in the length of time set forth above.

2. Wrecker-Salvager agrees to clean up the site of the building and agrees to remove all rubbish and debris except the removal of any foundations, and except as otherwise permitted herein: Exceptions:_____ _____

_____

3. Wrecker-Salvager shall have the right to salvage all materials taken from the building except as follows:

Exceptions: _____

4. The consideration in the amount set forth above in Paragraph 5 of the Recitals in the amount set forth in Paragraph 5 is to be paid by the person so stipulated to the person so named in Paragraph 5.

WAIVER OF LIABILITY AND HOLD HARMLESS

5. Wrecker-Salvager hereby agrees to waive any and all liability against the Property Owner for any actual or potential liability arising from accidents which occur during the demolition of the building.

6. Wrecker-Salvager further agrees that he shall hold the Property Owner harmless from any liability accrued as a result of injury to workman provided by the Wrecker-Salvager, or in the employee of the Wrecker-Salvager, or acting as his individual contractors.

7. All reference to Property Owner, Wrecker-Salvager, Contractor and length of time for completion of this contract hereto are incorporated by reference as the respective directions set forth in the Recitals set forth herein above.

8. PROPERTY OWNERS   WRECKER-SALVAGERS

   Date: _____   Date: _____

   _____   _____

   _____   _____

   _____   _____

about getting a barn or shed salvage job is that you may have competition from professional salvage crews which are combing the countryside these days looking for things to tear down. In some cities weathered barn siding sells for a higher price per board foot than new lumber. It's that much in demand for home paneling.

Wrecking can be dangerous. For this reason some owners are leery about letting amateurs do the job, fearing lawsuits. We've reprinted a Waiver of Liability (Demolition Agreement) which should calm the fears of the owner and make it easier to get the job.

The big hang-up on salvage jobs is the time involved. It looks easy and quick, but that's deceptive. It may take you a month of eight hour days to tear down a small house. When making the agreement try to get an extra month or two in which to complete the work. It would be wise also to try to get the work in the slow months of winter when your time is not at such a premium. You can keep warm over a fire of the splintered wood.

It may pay you to take a partner in the work. This is especially important if you do not have a truck, for you will need a partner who does. Not only will you need to transport your salvaged material home, but you are obligated to clean up the site after completion.

One last word here: be leery of those big jobs. Sometimes old brick schoolhouses or similar structures must be wrecked. When you hear the price that used brick is fetching in the cities your head may swim with figures of fortune. This is highly deceiving. The hidden costs of transportation and such are fierce. Though I've known of several people who have landed what looked like real plums, I've never known one who has come out ahead. I can't even recall a single instance where those who were hired to work on an amateur-run salvage job were paid in full.

Windows

Out in the countryside used windows have become hot property. A decade ago a guy could pick up a 24" x 30" window for 50¢. Now the running price is five to ten times that. Even old stained-glass church windows could be picked up for a dollar or two. Today the same window might start at $80 and run as high as $400 depending where it is sold.

Surprisingly, your best hunting areas for plain used windows may be the cities. Most every city has a wrecking-salvage yard or two. There is considerable wrecking that goes on in the cities and not much owner-building, so the price is often right. Sometimes outfits such as the Salvation Army, Goodwill or Saint Vincent DePaul sell old windows at a bargain. And don't shy away from storm windows and doors. The frames may not be as sturdy as a window built to open and close, and sometimes the glass is a little thinner, but they do a fine job when set in permanently. Buy windows whenever you can get them reasonably. If you wind up with too many you can always build greenhouses. They make fine swap items also.

Auctions

Out our way there is a "junk" auction every Thursday before the livestock sale. This is the homesteader's mainstay. Farmers from the area bring items that have been littering up their yards for years. Not only can you pick up building materials, you can also get excellent tools and household items at great savings. There is probably a similar sale somewhere in the vicinity of where you settle. If so, it could be worth driving fifty or more miles a week to attend. This is especially important when you are first settling in.

Farm auctions should not be missed either. This occurs when a family or old timer is leaving the land and selling out everything on the place. There are almost certainly building materials and tools to be sold, some of which are of a standard of quality no longer manufactured. Farm sales for as far as a hundred miles away may be advertised in your locality. Watch for handbills and ads in the paper. Get to the sale an hour or two early to check the condition of the merchandise and to decide how high you are able to bid on each item. Bring a lunch. It's usually a day long affair. Farm sales have the atmosphere of a carnival or of a picnic for everyone except the farmer who remembers how much he paid for each item originally.

Sawmill Lumber

Sawmills often are sources of free, or bargain rate, lumber. The day of the free mill-end (mentioned earlier) may be coming to a

where is the thicket?

Gone.

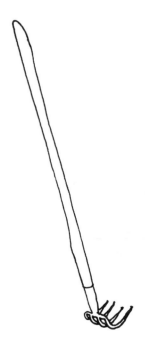

75

close at the larger mills where they are chipping them to make particle board, but there are sometimes other good deals. At some of the smaller eastern mills it is possible to get slabs which is the outer cut with the bark. Though these are not suitable for underground construction, they can make fine chicken coops or hog shelters and pens. Sometimes the mills will have stacks of the poorest grade lumber on sale for as low as $10 per thousand board feet. This material should not be used for roofing, but it might be suitable for the walls in underground construction if you keep the length of span down by using enough posts, or double the boards.

In the long run word-of-mouth may be the best way to gather material. You might want to start things off with a few signs on community bulletin boards and laundromats, or even with a small classified ad in the local paper, to let people know that you are seriously looking for material. Then begin talking it up. Ask people at auctions and at social events like potluck dinners if they know of lumber, windows and so forth which might be bought cheaply. And do not neglect your old-time rural neighbors. Gossip still rivals television as the main pastime in the country, and once the word gets out, the results, though slow, may be rewarding.

Polyethylene

As far as polyethylene goes we recommend buying it new. Old polyethylene which has spent even a few weeks in the sun tends to get brittle. After a few months in the sun it is all but worthless. The ultraviolet rays do it in. (This does not apply to polyethylene underground where it lasts indefinitely.) Secondhand polyethylene, if used at all, should go only into areas of secondary importance such as behind shoring outside firewindows or Royer Foyers, never behind the shoring in the house itself.

We used 4 mil on the $50 house, 6 mil on the $500 job. When we begin building these things commercially we'll probably go to an even heavier grade.

Concrete

If you are forced to build with concrete—to satisfy building codes, or because you are not in an area of abundant timber resources— you may be able to get four-fifths of your concrete for free from the local area. We're referring to the sand and gravel. The cement you will have to buy by the sack.

The sand must be what is known in the trade as "washed sand," that is, sand which is not salty. Ocean beach sand does not qualify. It may come from your own sand hill, or from that of a friendly neighbor. Or it may come from the bed of a stream. Watch this latter source, though. There are frequently environmental restrictions on the dredging of river bottom sand.

You might try to make friends with the local ready-mix concrete dealer and see if you can't enlist his sympathies. Those who mix and pour their own concrete these days are a rare breed and it's possible that you may receive his grudging respect. He will be able to tell you which sand type in the area is construction grade. He might even turn you on to a source. If nothing else, he should be good for advice on mixing and pouring.

There are many things to be said for using the services of a ready-mix outfit. The biggest advantage: by using a ready-mix outfit you will save countless hours of hard labor.

If you are determined to mix and pour your own, however, we offer this advice: do not attempt to mix the concrete by hand. You will regret it if you do. There are few construction jobs as tedious, as hard, and as time consuming as bending over a concrete trough all day with a shovel and mixing hoe. Concrete must be mixed thoroughly. It takes forever. And when you dump that first troughful into the forms it'll look like you've thrown a pebble into a volcano. We aren't talking about laying a few square feet of concrete around your suburban patio barbecue. We're talking here about pouring a *house*.

Concrete should also be poured as nearly continuously as possible for aesthetic reasons (cracks) and, more importantly, for strength of the unit being poured. For this latter reason alone I would never attempt to mix and pour a load-bearing roof by hand.

So you will need to buy, borrow, or rent a concrete mixer. This is not as tough a hurdle as it may sound. Since most everyone has gone to ready-mix there are numerous old concrete mixers standing out just rusting. Look around. You'll find one, and you'll find it cheap.

Free Timber Sources

We are going to assume here that the property you are planning to build upon is wooded, or at least that there are ample timber resources in the area.

The vast majority of timbered acres in the country today are cut-over forests. Of these, again, the vast majority need thinning. This includes both national forests and the small private timber holdings. We will grudgingly admit that the big timber outfits do thin their forests well (probably too well) which is the only good word you will find here regarding the timber interests.

Cut-over forests need thinning the way your garden needs weeding. When they are crowded together fighting for water and sunlight, trees not only do not grow well, they are more susceptible to disease and insect attack. So you should be open minded about selectively taking trees from your forest. Chances are it will do your woods nothing but good.

The fact that your trees have grown up crowded can work to your advantage when building. Crowded trees reach for the sun, growing tall as fast as possible to beat the competition. They don't put on much girth but this is an advantage to you since it means that there will be less taper. The result is that your posts and beams will be nearly as big at one end as at the other. That's nice. It's good material for your project. Crowded trees tend also to grow straight which is again greatly to your advantage. Nothing beats working with straight posts and beams. Finally, crowded trees tend to drop their lower branches where there is little sunlight. This means you have fewer knots to contend with and a higher quality lumber. (Woodsmen who want prime quality lumber deliberately trim the lower limbs during growth.)

If you don't have enough timber on your property there are several ways you might get it for free. One is to thin someone else's property in exchange for the material you take out. Unless there is a disease or insect infestation, the owner will want mostly the small trees removed. To avoid misunderstanding you might request that the owner mark the trees to be cut, or ask that the state forester do it. Timber with a diameter of six to twelve inches is prime material for posts and beams. Material larger than that may be milled for lumber. Material smaller may be used for fence rails and firewood. The small branches and needles or leaves should be left to rot on the ground at the logging site for fertilizer. These contain the greatest amount of soil building nitrogen of the entire tree.

A second free timber possibility is to log out the right-of-way for new private or county roads. If the road is to go through timber which is too small in girth to interest the commercial loggers it may be all yours for free. Even if there is commercial size timber you may be able to work in after the professional crews have creamed the best. By taking out the small trees you save the owner or the county the expense of bulldozing the trees in piles and burning them.

A third possibility is to salvage timber from a newly cleared field. You may pass a farm where the earth is raw and gashed by heavy equipment and where there are hundreds of yards, sometimes even miles, of rows of small timber and brush piled up by bulldozers. The farmer here is turning timber land into crop or grazing land and the piles are what he is going to burn when they have dried a little and weather conditions are right. If you ask he will usually let you take all you wish so long as you leave the remaining piles intact for burning.

A fourth possibility is to get the timber free from the national forest. Traditionally you are allowed sixteen cords of firewood per year per family by permit. At least out West. It used to be that they would also allow you enough logs to build a cabin and to fence your land, though they are tightening up somewhat these days. If anyone should see you at work and ask why you are taking your allotment out in lengths of eight, ten, twelve feet and so forth, you explain that you intend to buck them into firewood when you get home. Easier to haul this way. Fewer units to heave on and throw off the truck. Load rides better. Don't want chunks of firewood falling off and creating highway hazards. Tell them anything. They don't really care what you do with your allotment unless you sell it. Then they care a lot.

And what is
it to say
goodbye to
the swift
and the
hunt,

Milling Your Own Lumber

It is still possible in this day and age to take a load of logs in and have a large sawmill custom saw, kiln dry and plane it for you. If you got the stumpage for free and did the logging yourself you may save some money by this method. But you probably won't save a lot.

A better idea is to find someone in the area who has a small mill and work a deal. By doing so you should save considerable amounts. The small mill owner doesn't pay fancy union wages since he is often his only employee, usually doesn't have insurance costs, and pays nothing for transportation, marketing, storage and advertising of the product. You can air dry the lumber yourself. That may be a better method than kiln drying anyway.

There are more small owner-run mills than you might imagine. If asking around doesn't turn one up, an ad in the local paper probably will. You usually have to provide the stumpage and do the hauling, and if it is a one man outfit you may even have to provide half of the labor. All of this cuts down considerably on the cost.

It is even possible for you to buy your own small used sawmill. I've known of a few cases where complete rigs with circular saws went for as low as $40, though several hundred dollars is more common. Sometimes these small mills operate with diesel or gasoline engines, sometimes they are run with power take-offs from tractors.

If you are milling lumber for just one house, buying your own mill probably won't pay. If you are part of a community, though, it could be just the thing. What you have to watch for when buying is that you get a complete outfit. Lots of these small mills are in piles behind a farmer's barn and it is difficult for the untrained eye to tell if all of the components are there.

Probably the most common means these days for the owner-builder to mill his own lumber is with an Alaskan Mill. This is a contraption which holds a large chain saw and guides it by running down a straight 2x4 nailed to the log being milled. The special advantage of the Alaskan Mill is that it is the most portable of them all. You can carry it to the site as easily as you can carry the chain-saw. This allows you to mill right where you build, eliminating all transportation hassles. I'm taking a stab here, but I think with the cost of a good new saw you can set up the whole rig for around $500. And, of course, you will be using both the mill and the saw for years to come.

WORKING UP POSTS AND BEAMS
Sources, Seasoning and Peeling

You will need two types of structural timbers. The first type is for posts. This must be a wood which will take preservative well. It must have a certain amount of compressive strength. The second type is for the roof beams. This must have bending and shearing strength. Whether it will take preservative is not important.

For posts out our way we generally use cedar or lodgepole pine. Cedar is fine wood. It is light and easy to work. There are few knots and it peels well. Though our particular species doesn't, many cedars even smell great.

I've begun to favor lodgepole pine, however, for purely individual reasons. Though it is heavier, doesn't peel or work as well, and tends to be knottier, most of the lodgepole pines on my property are nearing maturity. Lodgepole pine has a short life span. It comes in quick after logging or after a fire and acts as a cover for the longer lived trees. It reaches maturity in 70 or 80 years. Then it dies off and other trees become dominant. Cedar, by comparison, takes two hundred years in Northern Idaho to reach maturity. They grow big around as the redwoods. I want to leave plenty of those giants to grow for my descendants to enjoy.

Find out what sort of timber the farmers in your locality use for fence posts, then use that species for the posts in your house. They should be using a species which takes treatment well, the possible exception to this being in extremely arid regions where farmers sometimes don't treat the fence posts at all.

If it is possible, use trees which are already dead. These will have seasoned (dried) already and will readily absorb the preservative, though if they have been lying on the ground you will have to get them up and let them dry some more. My favorite are snags (standing dead trees) which still have their

bark on. If dead long enough, these not only peel nicely, but usually have worm grooves cut into the exterior which are highly attractive. Naturally you won't want to use any timber which has rotted. Stick a sturdy knife into the wood to check for this. Watch the cedar. Often it will have rotted out in the center.

If you use living trees you will have to buck them to length and pile the posts off the ground to let them season. All wood which seasons quickly in this manner (as opposed to a snag which dries very slowly) tends to check. Checking means cracking. Though the checks look disturbing they are not really important. Beams which have checked lose little in the way of strength, posts lose virtually none. Those who build log cabins sometimes peel strips down the bark on opposite sides of a log. This way when the wood seasons it tends to check mostly along the peeled strips. The cabin is built so that the checking is straight up and straight down, covered by the chinking. If the checking were facing out it would provide an environment for insects, provide them with housing, so to speak. So would bark if left on the logs. Checking is relatively unimportant in our type of construction since underground housing attracts far fewer insects than one might imagine.

Still, you may not want your logs to check for aesthetic reasons. Several tricks are used to allow the wood to season slowly. One is to fall the trees in the late autumn or dead of winter so that the drying process is slowed. A second trick is to keep the bark on the logs during the seasoning. This latter suggestion has the disadvantage of making the material much harder to peel when you finally get to that stage. A newly dropped green tree peels well. One dropped during the spring sap flow peels exceptionally well.

Posts from trees dropped green in the winter will probably need at least six months to season. They must be stacked *up off the ground* during the seasoning process. If you are rushed you may have to drop the trees in the spring or summer and peel them right away. Even here they will probably need a minimum of three months seasoning. It should be obvious then that preparing the posts is the first step in the process of building an underground house unless you

happen to be lucky enough to score already seasoned material.

You may peel the timber with either an axe or a peeling spud. The latter has the advantage of performing the job quicker and more easily. It is also easier to leave thin strips of inner bark on the post or beam when using a spud. An axe, on the other hand, offers the advantage of being a tool you will already possess. An axe makes it possible to chop into the wood exposing the grain. If you are peeling dried (but not rotted) bark with an axe it becomes almost impossible *not* to cut into the grain, in fact.

There is good reason to want to leave on some of the inner bark and/or chop into the grain: it looks nice. On the $500 house we left as much as one-fourth the inner bark on the tamarack (larch) beams. It adds character. It provides interest. It made it unnecessary to stain the beams, so attractive were they. I did varnish them (highly recommended). The varnish gives them a luster, almost a glow, which makes them look handsome and expensive. I used spar varnish—the real stuff —not the cheaper "wonder" plastic imitation your hardware man will probably recommend.

Most of the posts in the $500 house were lodgepole pine. These peeled with difficulty, the bark tending to cling. They also had a fair number of knots making it difficult to use the spud. We had to hack away at them with the axe taking all sorts of bites and chunks out of the wood exposing the grain. We thought it looked shoddy at first till we stained them. Then they looked beautiful. The stain brought out the grain. We used a walnut stain, though there may be better ones to use. The walnut was a little dark for our tastes, so we applied it as lightly as possible. After several coats of varnish the posts were as handsome as you could wish.

Post Treatment

The whole purpose of treating the posts is to make them resistant to rot when in contact with the damp earth. Only the part which actually is set into the ground should be treated.

To take treatment they must, first of all, be thoroughly seasoned. Damp wood will not absorb the preservative solution. They must also be free of all bark, both outer and inner,

the end of living and the beginning of survival.

Above: Sitting on the lower side of the elevation change table, Therese Hubbell plans a menu. **Upper Left:** Therese stirs a sauce while guest at barbecue windows samples mountain refreshment. **Upper Right:** Mary Hubbell fiddles around in the study (as viewed from original section).

Right: Building crew of '75. Royer at right wears hub cap. Such merriment is not uncommon when jovial underground builders gather.

in the area to be immersed in the solution. They must not have been varnished, shellacked or painted and should be clean of mud, dirt and so forth.

There are two commonly used methods of treating posts: pressure treatment and soaking. Pressure treatment is what the professional outfits use and need not concern us here. It takes special equipment. To soak posts all you need is one or two 55 gallon drums. One fellow I know applied treatment to his posts with a paint brush, but I can't recommend this. The point of soaking is to allow the preservative to penetrate deeply.

There are two common preservatives. Creosote is the oldest. It is famous for use on telephone and power poles. I've never used it myself and so can't give you any tips. Directions should be on the can. Creosote smells bad. Though this is mitigated somewhat by the fact that most of the treatment is buried, some of it is certain to be exposed.

I've been using what most of the farmers in our area use, a poison called Penta. It is mixed one part in ten with kerosene or stove oil. Sometimes for economy we use regular diesel. We cut off the top of a 55 gallon drum, fill it not more than 1/3 to 1/2 way full with the solution (because the posts will raise the level of solution by displacement) and cram as many posts into the drum as it will hold. Length of time for soaking varies from twelve hours to four or five days depending upon the temperature of the solution, dryness of the wood, its girth, and species being treated. Dry cedar six inches in diameter might only need twelve hours on a hot summer day.

SEE "UPDATE"

Lodgepole pine ten inches in diameter treated in the cool of autumn might need five days. When the treatment begins soaking up the post six inches or so by capillary action I generally pull them and add new ones. It will soak upward much more readily on cedar than on pine.

To keep the barrel from turning over from the top-heavy weight of the posts, bury it at least half way in the ground. Take two posts and set them in the ground close to the barrel and nail a cross piece between them. Rest the top of the soaking posts against this.

If you are going to sink the posts to a three foot depth in your house you will need two barrels welded together with the bottom cut out of one of them. Using one barrel you will only be able to soak them conveniently to a height of about two and a half feet.

Some will object to using a poison which will obviously leach into the ground. This is a reasonable objection. I've always felt uneasy on this point myself. Being an organic gardener I would never under any circumstances use poison treated posts in my solar-geo-thermal greenhouses. There is one alternative: you may heat treat the posts. That is, you may scorch them slowly over a fire. In arid regions this may be all you'll need. Fire hardened wood lasts considerably longer underground than untreated, though I can't imagine it lasting even half as long as poison treated posts. The construction technique to be explained shortly makes it possible to replace posts with a minimum of fuss and without disturbing the structure of the house.

We might understand if we knew what it was that the white man dreams, what *hopes he describes to his children on long winter nights,*

Chapter 7
CONSTRUCTION TECHNIQUES

Secret Construction Method

You are capable of building an underground house without prior building experience. I firmly believe this. I believe a fourteen year old boy could do it. I think a lady could do it. Someone handicapped could do it if he had help with the heavier structural timbers. It's even possible a few businessmen could do it.

Now I'm not writing with a forked typewriter. With PSP the job is simplicity itself. Except for around the doors and windows there's no carpentry more difficult than notching a beam. The bulk of the construction is simply a matter of peeling and bucking logs, laying out polyethylene, stacking boards one on another or nailing them to the roof beams and throwing dirt in and out of the right places at the right times.

Not only do you have the PSP system going for you but you have my secret construction method. That method, developed out of desperation, is called starting-here and working-over-that-way-taking-it-as-it-comes. Other people sometimes label it "bad carpentry" . . . but never mind, here's the way it works.

First, put off that tough part that has you stymied till last. Then, finally, when there is nothing else that can be done and the whole project is being held up due to lack of completion of that critical section . . . spend a day or two going swimming, fishing, etc. This serves several purposes: (1) It makes you regret "wasting" the time and (2) it allows your mind to fester.

Once you begin to worry about letting time slip through your fingers, you'll get desperate to finish the job. You'll be infused with a form of cheap courage which should give you enough motivation to actually tackle that seemingly impossible task. This is very important . . . just as it's important to allow your mind to fester.

Festering is that form of semi-conscious, semi-unconscious thinking we all fall back on when we don't really know what the hell we're doing. Since you won't be building with blueprints drawn up by a trained architect, and since you probably have only the foggiest notion of carpentry techniques, thinking is going to be the biggest and longest part of the job. If you try to sit down and reason it all out logically you're going to get a headache and become grumpy. Better to let it fester.

When you're sufficiently festered and truly desperate, you'll get back to the project. Maybe you'll grab a 2x4 or a post that you'll run clear up to a beam somewhere because somehow in the back of your mind you know that it'll make the door jamb sturdier if you put it in that way. So you nail the member in place, hold the door up against it to get a measurement, mark it, cut a piece to go above the door . . . and you are on your way. Pretty soon you'll have boards spiked in here, windows placed there . . . and when things don't fit you'll rip them out and try putting them in a different way. Failures won't put you on a downer once energy and enthusiasm are running high because, by Steven Gaskin, *something is actually getting done.*

A professional carpenter, see, looks at the job and thinks of it as a whole. He either works from blueprints or he has enough experience and confidence to be able to figure everything out in advance. We can't do that. Trying to do so only leads to feelings of defeat and despair. So think *bit by bit*. Handle each problem as it arises. Start-here-and-work-over-that-way-taking-it-as-it-comes.

Which, I might add, is the way to do your whole homestead. Sure, you have to think ahead on *some*, maybe even *most* things. If you don't you could easily plant your garden where, two months later, your septic tank must go. But *never* become discouraged by some distant and seemingly insolvable problem. It'll work itself out in time. So will immediate problems. Bypass them. Go on to something else. Let the problems fester.

Don't worry about bad looking carpentry, either. You aren't a pro. None of us are. Few things will be plumb, there will be awkward gaps and spaces here and there. If your handiwork isn't professional, be glad. Look at the results of most professional builders today; sterile, hollow, plasterboard, suburban, blah houses. Your place will have character. It'll be built with love.

THE EXCAVATION

Excavations may be made either by machine or by hand. Each method has its advantages, each its drawbacks.

The advantages to using a machine are speed and the great amount of hard labor saved. The disadvantages are the amount of damage it causes the surrounding environment, and cost. In some cases the cost element may be overcome.

The two most commonly used machines for making excavations this size are the cat (bulldozer) and the backhoe. Of the two, cats by far do the most damage. This is because a cat does not lift the dirt out, but *shoves* it out. To do this, and to pile it somewhere, the operator must use considerable space on at least two sides of the excavation. Everything in this space—bushes, trees, topsoil—gets ground beneath the tracks.

A backhoe takes bites of the earth and stacks it neatly to the side. It works from a stationary position with the hoe arm and bucket swinging freely above the earth. If it is rubber-tired, as some are, there is a minimum disruption of the surroundings. Unlike a cat, a backhoe can cut four almost vertical walls. It also does a neat, efficient job of water and sewer line excavations and of the drain field ditches sometimes needed for French drains.

Where a backhoe is disadvantageous is in length of digging time. It may be competitive with a cat on small excavations—say a 500 square foot house—and it may likely beat a cat when digging individual water or sewer lines, but on any job of over 500 square feet a medium sized or large cat is going to do the job in a much shorter time. At $20 per hour and up this can translate into considerable savings.

There are many more cats around than backhoes, which is another consideration. This applies especially to communities where there is a lot of logging. They're used to skid logs, make roads and clear firelines. Old cats, still somewhat in operating condition, may occasionally be bought for as low as $300, practically the price of scrap metal. Like all old pieces of machinery they can be great headaches. A cat which breaks down often winds up costing a logging outfit considerable money. So they get rid of them. If you could buy one of those old clunkers, keep it operating long enough to excavate a house or two, and sell it again at the same price, you could excavate your house for free. There are a lot of "ifs" in that plan, however.

A better idea might be to have a friendly neighbor do the excavating for you with his cat. Over the years two of my neighbors have offered to dig my houses with their machines for free. I rejected these kindly offers with thanks only because I didn't want cat tracks in my forest and the resultant destruction of the trees around the building sites. Had I built in open country, though, I'd have jumped at the opportunity.

You might not have neighbors as good as these. Or you might be too new to the area to be on such terms. There is still the possibility of hiring a neighbor with a cat to do the excavating for $8 or $10 per hour on the weekends. If he lives close enough to walk the cat over you could also save the cost of transporting it by truck or lowboy.

what visions he burns into their minds, so that they will wish for tomorrow.

83

Digging By Hand

In the end you may decide to dig by hand. This is reasonable if your earth is not too rocky, or doesn't consist of clay which will stick to your shovel, and if your house isn't to be large. Digging time on the $50 house was three weeks for one man digging 6 to 8 hours per day. It was a little more than twice that for the $500 job.

A guy should not try to dig that long in one day. On days when there were eight hours of digging done at my place it was divided up between two or three men. If you're working alone spread the shovel time out over the weeks. In the end you'll come out ahead, for there is a point during each day after which you will slow down, the point of diminishing returns. Better to jump over to another aspect of the job then, peeling posts, or gathering material, or even working in the garden. Myself, I usually dig for two or three hours in the cool of the morning when I'm fresh, then do other things for the rest of the day. If really pressed I'll add a second shovel session in the cool of the evening, but only if sufficiently fueled with beer. Pour a couple of quarts of high octane brew in me and for the next several hours I can throw dirt like a dragline.

There are certain secrets to digging which can double your output. One is NEVER SWING A PICK UNLESS YOU ABSOLUTELY HAVE TO. Unless you are in very rocky soil, or hardpan, you probably won't have to.

To avoid swinging a pick dig in level strips or sections which traverse the slope. When you have dug a three or four foot section level make a hole in one corner as deep as the blade of the shovel. Next extend the hole into a small trench the same depth along the wall that runs down the slope. Now stand facing the trench and place the blade of your shovel six inches, or whatever is comfortable, back from the cut. The blade should be positioned so that it will dig straight down into the ground which means that the handle should be tilted slightly forward over the ditch. Stomp the blade. Step on the top part of it and begin wiggling the handle to loosen the dirt. If it is tough digging you may have to stand on the shovel with both feet and ride it into the ground as you wiggle the handle. When it is as low as it will go, step back and

pull the handle slowly (so you don't break it) towards you and down. You should have broken off a good chunk of earth. Scoop it up in one motion and throw it out of the excavation or into a wheelbarrow. There will be considerable loose dirt left in the trench. *Leave that dirt where it is for the time being.* Position the shovel so that it slightly overlaps the bite you have just taken and repeat the process. Continue doing this until you have dug a swath as wide as your ditch, step back six inches and begin working a new row always facing what you've just excavated. Work back and forth until you reach the far end of the excavation. You will find that the loose dirt left in the ditch helps to keep the initial big bite on your shovel so you don't have to make a special effort to get it back on each time you pull down on the handle.

When you've reached that far wall step to one side and clean enough of the loose dirt out to give you standing room. Now, facing the same direction you have been the whole

time, bend over and begin scooping the loose earth out, working forward. The loose earth ahead will help you get an effortless shovelful each time much the way a piece of bread helps you load your fork during meals. You can scoop it up and into the wheelbarrow in one movement. You have never once stepped on the loose earth and it comes up sweet as you could wish. This is the gravy part of the job. When you reach the original wall, dig a small hole in the corner and begin again.

A second secret, applicable to hillside jobs, is NEVER PUSH A WHEELBARROW UP OUT OF AN EXCAVATION. You should have designed your house so that you have a Royer Foyer entrance on the downhill side, or an entrance through a gable, or at the very minimum, a firewindow. If so, the level of these will be as low as the lowest floor of the house (the possible exception here being the floor of the root cellar).

If the house is to have two or more levels, concentrate the digging on the upper levels first. You can roll the wheelbarrow out right over the lower levels which have yet to be dug. Then, when you begin on the lower levels, *excavate the lower entrances at the same pace you excavate the floor.* Roll the wheelbarrow out these entrances each time you dump it and you will never once have to push a loaded wheelbarrow *up* out of the excavation.

A third secret is, MAKE USE OF EVERY WHEELBARROW LOAD YOU DUMP. Since you already have the earth in the wheelbarrow and must dump it somewhere anyway, why not make use of it? We did so by sinking posts downhill some fifty or so feet from the house and putting rough shoring up. Then we dumped all of our surplus earth in behind this on the uphill side and made terraces which were the same level as the lower level of the house. The result is that you enter the house on the same level as the work-recreation-cooking area outside. No more climbing up or down. No more scrambling after rolling logs you have been bucking or chopping on the hillside either. No more fighting the pitch of the hill as you go about your business. The terraces have made hillside living a blessing, not an effort. Not many features of the house have added to its comfort as much as those terraces.

The shoring need not be elaborate. The only requirement is that it be strong enough

to withstand the pressure of the earth. We didn't even use polyethylene. We used dead fallen timber scrounged from around the land. Sometimes we split the bigger logs, other times we used smaller pieces of wood. Sometimes we even used brush as shoring between the posts. The only real mistake we made on this part of the project was in not sinking the posts deep enough. There was nothing to brace them against and, though still holding, they have tended to push out.

An especially nice feature came when we used some living trees rather than posts to hold the shoring. The trees not only help to retain the earth, they add greatly to the

And because they are hidden, we will go our own way.

appeal of the terraces and provide summer shade while at the same time being positioned out of the way.

By using the earth in this manner you put an end to the eventuality of unsightly piles of earth lumped here and there.

A variation of this, one which is highly recommended, is to build a PSP structure with windows facing downhill while using the uphill wall as terrace shoring. The roof should be especially sturdy since you will cover it with dirt and use it as part of your terrace. It would not do to have a dozen or so guests at your first barbecue disappearing into the earth with shrieks as the roof of the terrace structure collapses.

This structure could be used as temporary housing for you as you build the big house. Later it could be used for food or tool storage, as a chicken coop, as a hog house, as a milking parlor or in a number of other ways.

Some will perceive that what I am recommending here is (heaven help us) a First-Thought House, and one without an Uphill Patio at that. The back will doubtless leak, there will be entrances from only one side,

there won't be cross ventilation, balance of light . . . and so on. But I'm not recommending it for other than temporary human habitat, something to pull you through those first few months. This project should also give you an opportunity to practice your building skills where your errors will not much matter.

Our fourth secret is to USE THE EARTH FROM THE UPHILL PATIO TO COVER THE ROOF OF THE MAIN HOUSE. It is simplici-

ty itself to lob earth over the roof when you are digging from above. One motion then digs the patio, gets rid of the earth, and covers the roof all at once. This will be the last large amount of digging that you do.

This applies to only the uppermost portions of the Uphill Patio. The lower portions such as the barbecue area should be excavated when you do the main portion of the house and that earth may be removed by wheelbarrow and used for the downhill terraces. This is because the lower portions of the patio involve larger amounts of earth displacement than you will need on the roof. It would also be tough to throw dirt from those lower sections up over the roof.

You should remember to reserve the top two to four inches of earth on the roof for the top soil which you took off at the beginning of your excavation and cleverly piled to the side. This soil which you took off first will go on last, in other words. It will greatly aid in the revegetation of the roof. Don't worry about leaves, pine needles, twigs and such. They make fine mulch and humus.

Our fifth and final secret is IN TOUGH DIGGING SITUATIONS, BLAST. This seems scary but it is actually pretty safe if you use a few simple precautions such as not smoking around the dynamite, not crimping the blasting cap with your teeth and the like. It is a rush to work with powder. It is also surprisingly inexpensive and most effective.

Virtually the only tools needed are a blasting auger to dig the hole and crimping pliers. You may even be able to borrow both of these. We figured it out once, and the cost of powder, blasting caps and fuses came out to a matter of pennies per wheelbarrow load of earth—a great bargain if it keeps you from swinging a pick. Most every rural town has a hardware store which sells dynamite and caps. You will want ditching powder as opposed to stumping powder. Remember to tamp dirt back in the hole after you lower the stick in. Need we advise you to run like hell and get down behind something once you've lit the fuse? If it doesn't blast give it an hour or so before you go digging it up because sometimes the fuses smolder.

BUILDING THE STRUCTURE

One of the places where amateurs often, and professionals occasionally, bungle a construction job is on the building procedure or sequence. Certain things have to be completed before other steps in the process are begun. Otherwise there can be heavy difficulties.

An example of this comes to mind quickly. A friend, an amateur, was building a house for his in-laws in Bolinas, California in 1967. I walked over one day to see how he was doing. He seemed to be doing well, was just finishing up laying the hardwood floor. I didn't see any pipes or water lines coming up through the floor, however, and I asked about this.

"Haven't put them in yet," he said.

"You mean not up through the floor yet, or nothing laid there at all?"

"Nothing at all. I was figuring on doing that last."

"You haven't even dug the ditches under there yet?"

"No, why?"

"Because that's the first thing you do after pouring footings. You call that roughing-in the plumbing. You dig your sewer and water ditches and lay the pipe. THEN you do the floor. Otherwise, like now, you have to crawl around on your side or stomach in that little crawl space and try to dig the ditches and lay the pipe that way. This earth around here is what we call hardpan clay, which is why no one's septic tank drains well. That clay is so tough we usually have to use a jack hammer on it. Now there's no room to do that or even to swing a pick."

Several years of roughing-in sewer lines on construction jobs in that county made me shake my head sadly at the thought of his difficulties ahead. I made the mistake then of muttering, "I'm sorry I didn't get over here earlier to see how you were doing," and was rewarded with a look of accusation which haunts me to this day.

So the sequence is important. Here is the suggested building procedure for PSP underground houses:

(1) Build downhill terrace shoring and/or temporary habitation.
(2) Dig hole (using earth to make terraces).
(3) Get approximate floor heights using a line level.
(4) Set corner posts.
(5) Set other posts one at a time.
(6) Notch in and bolt roof girders.
(7) Notch in and spike super beams and roof beams.
(8) Put in French drains, if used.
(9) Rough in plumbing lines, electrical conduits, if used.
(10) Put on roofing boards.
(11) Build walls, cabinets, closets, etc.
(12) Finish roof and Uphill Patio excavation.
(13) Put in windows and doors.
(14) Install carpet anchors.
(15) Tamp floor, rough smooth it.
(16) Pour concrete base for toilet, bath or shower.
(17) Install plumbing and lighting fixtures.
(18) Finish floor, lay carpets.
(19) Install stove.

We are going to examine these points one at a time giving the reason for the sequence. We'll also try to explain thoroughly just what it is that you do during each of these steps.

Steps (1) and (2) have been well explained in the preceding pages on excavation. We'll make just one further observation here. Many people, when digging by hand, tend to let the sides of their excavation taper. If your earth is holding well, not caving in or crumbling down, you should avoid this. Your sides should be as vertical as possible. Though it often seems a nuisance, or an extra effort to do this, it actually *saves* you labor. You can only build as large a house as the floor is wide. Since your posts are going to stand straight up, any tapering back that the earthen wall does represents unused excavation, or work that you have done for nothing. If you try to eliminate the taper when nearly done digging you'll likely find you have to swing a pick. So shave those walls vertical as you dig.

The reason for (3) *making your floor level* at this step is so that you have a true idea of how deep to sink your posts. On a large house it is entirely possible for one end to be as much as a foot higher than the other when you eyeball it during construction. If you sink your posts under these conditions you are going to have to add a foot of earth later to the low side which would not only negate a foot of your hard digging and raise the floor a foot

If we agree, it will be to secure your reservation you have promised. There, perhaps we may live out our brief days as we wish.

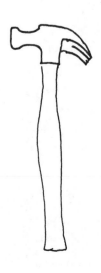

more than you wanted it, but also add up to a foot of earth around the untreated portion of the posts causing rot. A more reasonable alternative would be to excavate a foot from the high side. This however has the disadvantage of exposing treatment within your house where it might possibly smell or where young children may touch or even chew on it. Excavating would also make the post less sturdy. The final possibility would be to leave the floor at a slope beneath your carpet. Doing this will cause you no end of future annoyance. Your house will seem most unprofessionally built. You'll notice it for

sure. All of the hassle can be avoided by leveling the floor at this point.

(4) *Set the corner posts.* You must set the corner posts first so that they can become guides for the other posts both in height and position.

There are a number of steps to setting a post correctly. First you must dig a hole with a post hole digger (greatly recommended over a shovel) which is wide enough to allow the handle of a shovel to fit around the post on all sides during the tamping process. Next, using a level, you must make sure the posts are vertical, and that they stay vertical during tamping. This involves either continually checking while working, having a friend hold the post, or nailing several boards like legs to the post to support it.

Begin tamping by shoveling dirt back into the hole not more than a fourth or a third of the way up. Turn the shovel upside down and pound that loose earth (tamping) so that it becomes compressed or solid (compaction). Shovel another six to ten inches of earth in and repeat the tamping. Do this until you reach the top. If the earth is very dry you may want to dampen it as dry earth compacts poorly. Tamping is important not only because it keeps the post from wiggling later, but because it also provides resistance which helps to keep the post from sinking from the weight of the building above. Another trick to keep it from sinking is to throw as large a rock as you can into the hole before dropping in the post. Being larger than the diameter of the post the rock will help to disperse the weight. It should also help to keep the end of the post from rotting out.

When all the corner posts are in place you should trim them for height. (Presumably you have used posts which have excess length.) Pick out a post on the lower wall, decide how high you want it to be, mark and trim. Using a line and line level find the same height on the other lower corner post. Mark and trim. Repeat the process for the upper wall.

Chris and Steve talk over structural problem.

88

(5) *Set other posts one at a time.* Use the corner posts for guides. Do this by running a line from the top and another near the bottom of the corner posts of the same level connecting them. These lines must be on the *outside.* Your posts will doubtless be of different diameter. If you try to line them up so the inside surfaces are in line, then the shoring itself will undulate from post to post.

To *set the middle posts* follow this sequence: First run the lower line across. Measure where the posts are to go and drop the line to get it out of the way. Dig the holes remembering that they must extend towards the wall past the line (so that you may get the shovel handle in during the tamping). String both lines and drop a post in one hole. If the hole isn't right pull the post and make corrections. Drop the post in again and line it up so that it almost but not quite touches the two strings. This will give you your forward and back plumb, plus the correct position. Check your right and left plumb with a carpenter's level. Begin backfilling and tamping as outlined above checking for plumb as you work. Repeat the process individually for each of the other posts. Trim using the top line as a marker.

(6) *Notch in and bolt girders.* We built our houses using two different systems. On the $50 house we ran girders across the top and lower wall posts, connected them with what we called "super beams" then notched in our roof beams. A simpler method, the one which we used on the $500 house, was to simply run the girders directly from the high wall posts to the lower wall posts, then put on the roof beams.

You may either nail the posts to the girders, or, preferably, you may bolt them. Bolting has the advantage of allowing easier replacement of the posts in sixty or seventy years when they begin to rot out on the bottom.

To replace one you need merely roll back the carpet and polyethylene, jack up the beam slightly on either side, dig a hole in front and beneath the post and pull it down and out. With our system the retaining/shoring is not nailed to the post so the wall doesn't come out with it. The wall should remain in place so long as you replace the posts singly. The new post must be notched the same dimensions as the old one and a new bolt hole drilled. Then it should be

slipped into place and the earth tamped firmly beneath. Tamp more earth back around, smooth it to floor level, let down the jacks and replace the polyethylene and carpeting.

The process is slightly more difficult if the posts have been nailed. Ripping out the old nails and replacing them with new ones may gouge the girder some, but it is still feasible.

By this process all of the posts in the house may be replaced without disturbing the walls or roof, both of which should last nearly as long as the polyethylene which, as we have said, is expected to last indefinitely underground.

and the memory is only the shadow of a cloud moving across the prairie,

(7) *Notch in and spike super beams and roof beams.* There are several important things to point out here. The first is that you must put the beams in before doing the work on the walls. If you attempt to do the walls first, the pressure of the earth as you tamp the backfill will push the posts in. They will no longer be plumb. It will happen slowly, but it will happen. The end result will be posts and walls which teeter in at unpleasant, almost threatening angles. The only correction for this is to dig out completely behind the walls, pull the posts and begin again.

The girders, beams and super beams transfer the pressure from one wall all the way across the house to the other wall. This is the second thing we are pointing out here. It is one of the secrets of the PSP construction system. All pressure—lateral thrust and hillside creep—is counterbalanced by pressure from the opposite side of the house. This is why we haven't recommended putting in diagonal bracing which is so important to the structural integrity of frame houses. There is no need for it on a properly built PSP underground structure.

It is for this reason that we emphasize notching the posts, girders and beams. Notching vastly increases the strength of these members at the points of union. Nails, spikes and bolts alone will not suffice. With the weight of a whole hillside pushing on them nails and bolts may pull out, bend or shear. They will hold firm when notched.

There is a possibility still that the whole structure may be forced out of plumb when tamping the back fill behind the first wall if that wall is completed before the opposing wall is begun. This could probably only happen if you were using a mechanical tamper. Professional builders take note. To avoid this build up the opposite wall a few feet and tamp behind for counterpressure.

It is difficult to imagine the whole structure going out of plumb when the tamping is done by hand. If this should happen it is indicative of posts not sunk deep enough or tamped well and of girders and beams poorly joined. In that case your whole structure is in trouble.

(8) *Put in French drains.* These must go in on the outside before the walls go up because they are at the very bottom. If the French drain is to go all the way up a wall towards the surface you will obviously have to do that part in conjunction with placement of the wall itself.

Where the French drain is in contact with the polyethylene on the outside of the wall there is a problem, especially if the fill is crushed gravel. The problem is that the rock may tear the polyethylene. To solve this

Chris on top of structure, as Steve and Marilyn watch. Roof beams have yet to go on. Planks on top are to facilitate work.

90

dilemma three approaches may be taken. First you may stack the fill in the trench in sacks, such as burlap bags or sand bags. This might be a nice neat way of doing it. It would obviously be an expensive way unless you have access to free bags. A cheaper method is to place cardboard against the polyethylene when you shovel in the fill. Flattened old cardboard boxes will do. Even so, shovel with care.

The combination of crushed gravel and polyethylene makes me nervous. Here the third method should be used. This is to fill the drain trench slowly and try to put four or so inches of sand or other soft earth against the polyethylene itself, the gravel outside.

(9) *Rough-in the plumbing lines and electrical conduits.* If you are going to utilize these luxuries this is the stage in which the initial work must be done.

In the case of the plumbing it is not crucial at this point. You could tunnel the water and sewer lines out under a door or wall of windows such as at a Royer Foyer later if you choose, though it would be a minor hassle. In the case of the electrical conduits, however, the timing is essential.

The conduits must be placed now before the walls go up. The only alternatives later are to either dig out the walls from behind or string the wiring inside the house. This does not apply to the conduits which are to be laid along the roof. These must obviously be placed after the roof boards are up.

We make a humble suggestion here, one which many homesteaders may choose to ignore. It is this: If you aren't going to electrify, at least consider putting a few conduits up behind your walls in case you should want to electrify later. It is simple to do. Just run a few plastic pipes up your walls and cut in blank outlets when the walls go up during the next two steps. You need not run the conduits under the floors now; that may be done in later years, but the wall conduits could be a tremendous saving in labor if and when you do decide to go electric. Electricity may be unnecessary in your youth but in your senior years it could be important. The conduits could also add to the resale value of your house.

It is beyond the scope of this book to instruct you on plumbing and electrical work. Your local library should have helpful materi-al. If not, check the Whole Earth Catalog. Even Sears has pamphlets which will tell you how.

(10) *Nail on roofing boards.* While most of the wall boards will not require nails, the roof boards definitely will. They won't have the pressure of the earth immediately on them to hold them in place as do the walls. They could conceivably slip while you walk over the roof during construction. They might pop out of place during an earthquake causing devastation to those below, whereas if the wall boards were to pop out there would not likely be more than a foot or two of earth coming in. The nails should add something to the strength of the structure. A final reason for nailing the boards on the roof, but not the walls, is that you have room to swing a hammer whereas on the walls of a hand dug house you probably won't.

The roofing boards may either be the length of one span between two posts or they may be longer. The advantage of using longer boards is strength. There are several advantages to using shorter boards. One is that you may use bits and pieces that commercial builders and sawmills throw away as too short. The second advantage is that shorter boards may make a snugger roof. If the roof beams vary in diameter as they doubtless will, and if your notching of the beams is uneven as it doubtless will be if you are not a professional carpenter, then the top of your roof beams will show variation in height. This is to say that if you have three beams and the two outside ones are higher than the center one, then trying to span the three with one board might not be entirely successful. From below the board may appear to have pulled away from the center beam. This could be true even with the weight of the earth on the board. It makes a bad looking job. Shorter boards, spanning just from center to center of the beams do away with this difficulty.

The roof beams should be flattened to give a surface of at least several inches to nail the boards upon. The plane of these flattened areas should be at the same angle as the pitch of the roof. If you have an Alaskan Mill you may make this trim before putting the beams in place. Otherwise a broad axe or an adze will do the job after the beams are up. This latter method has the advantage of making

for they love this earth as the newborn loves its mothers heartbeat.

the plane more likely to conform with the pitch of the roof since the notching process has already been completed.

When the boards are nailed in place, run your electrical conduits up the roof for any ceiling fixtures you might want. They should be run up the roof rather than across. This facilitates drainage. Anything lying across the roof will bunch the polyethylene above it creating a moisture trap. The principle of never letting water back up anywhere against the house is doubly important on the roof.

You might want to build a casing around the electrical conduit (if you have access to a table saw) to keep the building paper and polyethylene from stretching over it from the weight of the earth and possibly tearing. The sides of the casing should be beveled so that there are no sharp or abrupt edges.

Care should also be taken so that the roof boards are smooth without large gaps or holes that may also allow the building paper and polyethylene to stretch in time and tear. If you build with new lumber (ship-lap preferred) there should not be much problem on this score. Building as I do with imperfect lumber I often have to patch around holes and cracks. Over large gaps I tack window screen which is then pounded flat so that there are no sharp edges. To smooth out irregularities between boards I mix up concrete and trowel it on.

When all of this is completed apply building paper, always remembering to overlap the upper piece over the lower in the manner of shingles so that the rain will run off.

Somewhere in here you must build shoring above the windows and doors to retain the earth. These should be several inches higher than the desired depth of the earth on the roof. You will not need to build shoring above solid walls. There the earth on the roof merges with the earth surrounding the house.

It is not crucial to do this portion of the roof at this time. If you do, however, it will keep the rain or possibly hot sun off you when you work on the walls.

(11) *Build the walls, cabinets and closets.* You might try to complete the downhill wall first so that the runoff from the roof is conveniently conducted downhill rather than dribbling into the construction area causing mud.

Here are the steps to follow when building a wall:

Begin by digging a trench along the outside of the posts the length of the wall. This trench should be two to four inches deeper than the eventual level of the floor. It must be wider than the width of the boards you will use on the bottom. It should be flush with the outside of the posts. Make sure that the ditch is level from one end to the other.

Now stretch out the polyethylene making sure that there is plenty of surplus. At the bottom you will want eighteen inches or more extra so that the polyethylene may wrap under the lower board and come out to extend a foot or more under the floor poly providing a moisture and dust barrier. There must be enough extra at the top to allow the polyethylene to underlap the polyethylene from the roof. You will want extra there also because the polyethylene tends to pull down during the backfill. You may lose a foot or more this way during the construction of a six foot wall. Give yourself plenty extra to work with until you get the hang of it. The polyethylene should also extend around the corners by at least a foot so that it may overlap that of the other walls.

Measure and cut a board so that it reaches from center to center of the first two posts. Lay it in the ditch with the polyethylene coming up on either side. *Make sure the board lies level in the ditch.* If it does not, pull it and make corrections beneath the polyethylene. When the board is level stretch the polyethylene up behind it and shovel some dirt in back and tamp. Repeat this process between the other posts, always remembering to use a level on these first boards because if these go in crooked, the rest of the boards up the wall will be crooked.

The polyethylene which is in front of the boards, about a foot of it, will have bunched up around the posts. Take a knife and slit it so that it will come around the posts and lie flat on the floor.

Now begin building up the walls laying one board at a time, backfilling, stretching the polyethylene, tamping and working across the wall so that all sections rise together. When earth begins to spill out the corners it is time to begin another wall if that corner is not to be in windows or doors. If it is, you will have to rig up shoring there.

Where one earth backed wall meets another the polyethylene must overlap. Polyethylene from the upper wall should overlap on the outside of that of the side walls and the polyethylene of the sidewalls should overlap that of the downhill wall. This is done so that there is no edge of poly exposed to the dirt facing uphill to catch the water seeping down. Stop construction when you are a foot or more from the roof so that the roof polyethylene may overlap all the wall poly.

During this stage you should be building in cabinets, closets and shelves. These are built right into the wall and are another of the advantages of underground housing for you may build as many as you wish. With an aboveground house you can't do this or the house would look strange indeed from the outside with various lumps and protrusions.

The closets, cabinets and shelves need not have the structural integrity of the remainder of the house since you are not going to live in them, yet they must be built to withstand the lateral pressure of the earth. This is achieved by overlapping the backboards over the sideboards so that the earth pressure is transferred from the back to the side to the posts against which the whole unit rests. Shelves and cupboards may be built with one inch lumber but the closets being bigger should be built with two inch. It is important when laying out the polyethylene to remember to leave enough to wrap comfortably around these additions to the walls. The only other

important thing to know here is that the ceilings of the closets and the tops of the shelves and cabinets must be sloped to allow water to run off. You may find that you have to do additional digging into the earthen wall to make room for these units. If so, the newly excavated earth may be used immediately as backfill for the other sections of the wall.

Plumbing lines and electrical conduits should remain on the inside of the polyethylene. The hot water lines may be insulated to keep the poly from melting but otherwise no other special efforts need be made. You do not need to encase the conduits along the walls as you do on the roof. Remember to cut openings in the wall boards for these lines as you build. Install the switch and outlet boxes and connect them with the conduit. Running the wire can come later.

When using the polyethylene on the walls remember that too much is far better than too little. It matters little if the poly bunches up

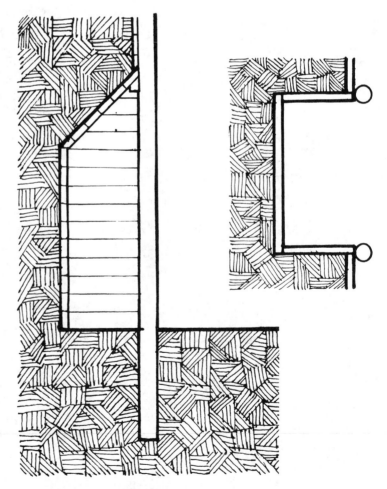

Closet and cupboard built with overlapping boards to withstand pressure of earth.

Neighbor Ricky Hudson demonstrates first three steps in building a wall. At right he digs a narrow, shallow ditch behind the posts. At lower left he places the board and levels it. Lower right he begins stretching out the polyethylene by first pulling the board then tucking poly under, leaving about a foot of overlap. Before placing any more boards he will again check the first board for level.

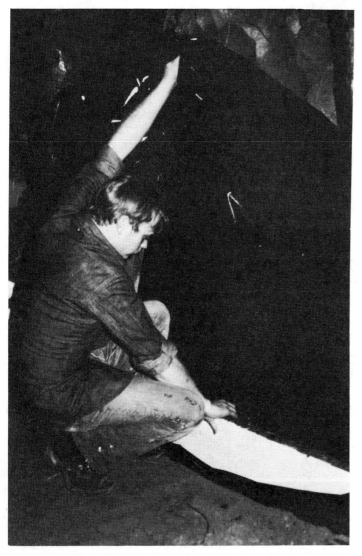

along the walls but it matters a great deal if it is under strain, such as around the inner corner of a closet or shelves. Never allow the polyethylene to take the strain of holding back earth by itself.

We will emphasize again that when back filling and tamping behind a wall the polyethylene must be pulled up constantly.

A last item, one which is so obvious we have overlooked it: The polyethylene is a moisture barrier, an absolute one, but it can remain so only if it is not pierced, torn or punctured. This means you must never staple or tack it in place. Sometimes to hold it temporarily in position you may thumbtack it at the top edge, but only if that section is to be overlapped with other poly. If you are joining two pieces as, say, on the roof, they must be overlapped and taped with wide, heavy plastic tape. On the $50 underground house we used 4 mil poly but on the $500 one we used 6 mil. Get it in rolls 20 feet wide.

(12) *Finish roof and Uphill Patio excavation.* You have already nailed on the roof planks, smoothed abrupt contours, and rolled out building paper. The next step is to spread out the first layer of polyethylene.

Sweep the building paper to remove any foreign matter. Roll out the polyethylene and cut it so that there is at least a foot of overlap on the sides and downhill wall. On the uphill side, you will need additional surplus because the polyethylene will slide down when you begin to apply the earth. How much surplus depends on the pitch of the roof, how long it is, and how much is anchored with earth on the sides where it has overlapped the wall poly (some parts of the roof will be over windows and doors) and how often you pull it up from above. On a twenty foot roof you might be safe with three to four feet extra. If it should happen that you err on the long side, so much the better. If you err on the short side you will have to cut additional and overlap it from the top making a "boot."

Finish off the last foot or so of walls, overlap with the roof poly, back fill and tamp. Now begin *gently* applying four inches of the cleanest rock-and-stick-free earth you can find. Do this a shovelful at a time working up from the bottom. Use dry earth if you can on this layer. It has far better insulating qualities

than that which is damp. As you apply the earth pull up on the poly from above as frequently as you can stand. Tacking it doesn't work; it just tears. Best if you can have one person constantly pulling as two others apply the earth. You are not only trying to save polyethylene, you are trying to get it to lie as flat and wrinkle free as possible so that there are no creases to catch and retain water.

Top: Stretching the first layer of polyethylene for the roof. **Bottom:** Applying the first layer of earth.

95

When the earth is on, rake it smooth with the back of a garden rake pulling out any sticks, twigs or other sharp objects you spot. Roll out the second layer of poly. Cut it so that there is surplus as before, only this time the surplus is to lie out flat on the ground rather than overlapping the wall poly. It is hoped that several feet of polyethylene buried out beyond the walls will escort moisture down the hill rather than letting it soak in near the walls. Not only might this help to prevent leaks, it will also help keep the soil near the walls dry thereby increasing the insulating qualities of the earth.

Incorrect procedure for raking first layer of earth smooth is demonstrated here. Tines of rake should not be used, but backside, so as not to risk tearing polyethylene.

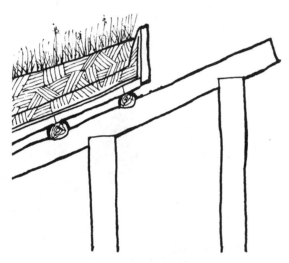

Incorrect method of finishing upper portion of roof. This was one of the original mistakes on the $50 house. Despite author's most vigorous efforts (grooves, sealers) water continues to run down beam and into house. Rain also runs down retaining board and enters between edges of roof/ceiling planks.

Correct method of designing roof. There is no slanted beam out in the weather to catch the rain. Design also incorporates a *drip board*, an extension of the shoring which hangs low and allows water to drip off rather than run down between roof/ceiling planks and into house.

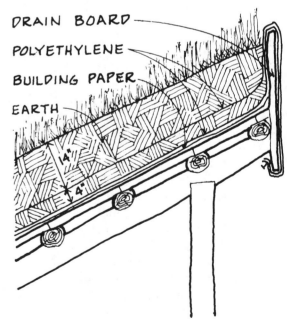

DRAIN BOARD
POLYETHYLENE
BUILDING PAPER
EARTH

The second layer of polyethylene is a safety factor. If somehow the lower layer should tear or perforate you have the layer above as a moisture barrier. If they should both get holes you have that four inches of earth to absorb the moisture and disperse it so that the water hopefully will not congregate around the lower hole. Even a pinprick will allow considerable entry if water has collected above it.

Weight down the edges of the second layer with clumps of earth so that a breeze doesn't play havoc with your work. (Don't try to spread polyethylene on the roof in a high wind. Besides the incredible hassle, you run a risk of perforations.) Shovel on three or four inches of as fine, sharp-object-free earth as you can scrape up. Remember to keep pulling up on the polyethylene as before. Once the protective layer of soft earth is in place you may begin covering the roof in earnest by throwing earth over the top as you dig out the Uphill Patio. Eighteen inches is a good total amount of earth for a roof. Make the last several inches the top soil which you piled along the sides at the beginning of the excavation. Sow some seeds at this point if you wish and cover with mulch. Trim the excess polyethylene from the top (use it behind the shoring on the Uphill Patio). Lay boards over the edge of the polyethylene and nail it to the top of the roof shoring to keep rain from working under.

Your roof is now complete. Stay off it as much as possible for the first month or two until the earth compacts of its own weight. If seeds you may have sown do not grow well, don't fret. It is difficult to get domestic plants to grow on the roof because there is no ground moisture for them to draw upon. Ma Nature will take care of the situation for you. In several years your roof will be lush with vegetation.

love it as we've loved it.

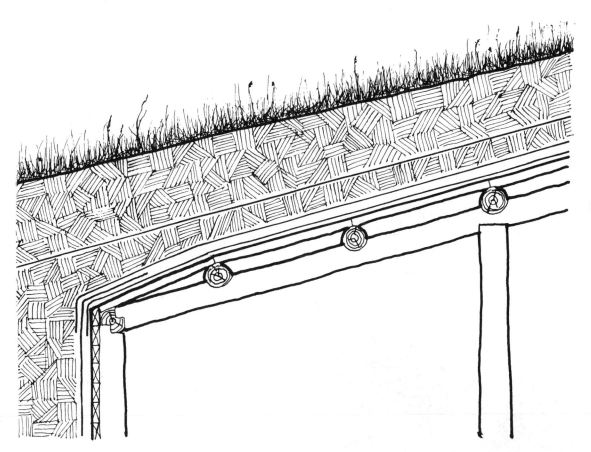

Detail of beam and post notching, wall and roof planking and polyethylene layers.

Care for it as we've cared for it.

(13) *Put in windows and doors.* Do this step *after* digging out the Uphill Patio or rocks and clods of earth may roll down and crash through your windows.

Don't look to me for advice on finer carpentry. I have a time of it here myself. Either get competent help, or find material in your local library or book store, or the Whole Earth Catalog. Even the U.S. Government Printing Office used to have material which would tell you how. They may still.

(14) *Install carpet anchors.* Carpet anchors are another of our "inventions." They are 2x4's or 2x6's set into the earth flush with the floor level adjacent to the lowest wall board. This is what you tack your carpet to for a smooth job.

If a professional crew is to lay your carpets check with your dealer to see if there is something more to add to the anchors. Many of the pros have a special way of hooking the rugs.

15. *Tamp floor, rough smooth it.* Assuming that you don't have access to a gas driven or compressed air tamper you will have to tamp by hand with a 2x4 or something similar.

Not all of the floor will need tamping—just where you have done any digging. When I built my $500 house I built a root cellar into the upper elevation with an entrance from

the lowest elevation. The roof of the cellar is part of the floor of the level above. Though I thought I'd done a competent job of backfilling and tamping around the walls of the cellar, time has shown this to be untrue; during the past several years the earth there has sunk as much as three inches making an annoyingly unlevel floor. Guess I hadn't tamped carefully enough during the backfill. When time and energies allow, I'll have to roll up the carpet and correct matters.

(16) *Pour concrete for toilet, bath or shower.* All of these must have solid concrete bases on which to stand. For a job this small it is possible to mix the concrete by hand in a trough or wheelbarrow. It's probably not worth your time to try to scrounge material for this little a job. Buy sacks of concrete mix.

(17) *Install plumbing and lighting fixtures.* See item (13) for advice on this.

(18) *Finish floor, lay carpets.* Finishing the floor is an art in itself. It is difficult to get it completely smooth, but smooth it must be. It took me three days to lay the carpets in my place and most of that time was spent smoothing out the floors.

Begin by taking off any obvious lumps with a shovel and filling in depressions. Stamp down the new fill with your feet. Run checks to make sure that it is the same level on one side of the room as the other. Lay a straight 2x4 on the earth and look underneath for high and low spots. Correct these with a shovel or garden rake. Next take the rake and rough up the whole surface. Smooth it out with the back side of the rake. Now take an unwarped 2x6 and drive several big nails in deep enough so that they will hold but not so deep that they go through the other side. Use the nails as handles and begin finishing the floor as a cement finisher works concrete. This is slow, painstaking, tedious work but it must be done. Any irregularities in your floor will become apparent shortly after you lay your carpets. They will annoy you for years afterwards.

Laying carpets is an art also and one which I have not mastered. It is difficult to cut the carpets correctly to fit them around the posts along the wall. In the case of posts in the center of the room you have your hands full. You are going to have to lay the carpets in strips in the latter case which means putting in long

Finishing floor.

98

carpet anchors down the center of the floor. Your carpet dealer will custom cut the rugs to your specifications at the store if you can give him the exact dimensions.

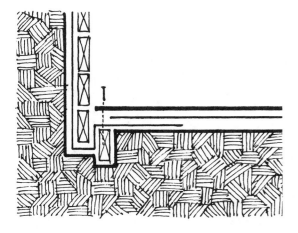
Detail of carpet anchor and overlapping polyethylene.

Before laying the carpets you should put down a layer of polyethylene and have it overlap the polyethylene coming up from under the walls. This not only acts as a moisture barrier to help preserve the carpet (never lay a wool carpet without it) but it will help keep any dust from working up through the material.

(19) *Install stove*. When you complete this step your house is a true home.

We can't advise you here as to what type of stove to use. It depends on such factors as your funds, the size of the house, and what kind of fuel you intend to use.

Me, I've just been using the cheapest of wood stoves all of these years, the type which is referred to as an air tight heater. These are made from sheet metal and will burn through in a winter or two of hard use. I would have gone to a quality stove long ago if I could have afforded it. Fisher is one brand which has caught my eye. Wood stoves are a reviving technology. They reached the peak of efficiency around the turn of the century, then began to wane as other fuels became popular. Today they are making a strong comeback.

I laid brick for a special flooring around my stove. I also designed it so that I had about eighteen feet of stove pipe running up near the slant roof. This latter was to allow me to recover every possible calorie of heat before it went up the smoke stack. It worked. Unfortunately, however, we must usually burn soft woods that create a lot of creosote, which is not only a fire hazard, but also clogs up the pipes and—even worse—eats them through like acid in a year's time. A good efficient stove, lots of seasoned hardwood and a shorter stove pipe would make my life easier. Not complaining, mind you. I'd take even my troublesome system over oil, gas, or electrical heat any day. Wood fires have soul.

Chapter 8
YOU AND THE BUILDING CODES

Now we come to the most difficult question in the book. Will a home built with the PSP system pass the code? The answer is, sadly, no.

You are going to have to sit down and figure some way out, through or around this hurdle. If it is any consolation there are lots of other folks, whether they are building above or below ground, who are facing the same problems. All owner-builders in code areas do.

You may grope for an answer to this dilemma through one of five possible avenues.

YOU MAY MOVE TO AN AREA WHICH HAS NO CODES.

YOU MAY BUILD UNDERGROUND WITH CONCRETE OR OTHER SOCIALLY APPROVED MATERIAL AND BRING THE HOUSE UP TO CODE.

YOU MAY TRY TO GET A CODE VARIANCE FOR YOUR HOUSE.

YOU MAY TRY TO GET AN UNDERGROUND HOUSE AMENDMENT TO THE CODE.

YOU MAY EVADE THE CODE THEREBY BECOMING AN OUTLAW BUILDER.

MOVING TO AN AREA WHICH HAS NO BUILDING CODE

This upon first glance seems like the easiest, most sensible solution to the problem. It might even work. On the other hand it might not, either. If not, it will leave you embittered and frustrated beyond description.

Why might it not work? Because *one by one the various areas are adopting the code.* It is quite possible for you to buy land, and in perhaps the six months it takes you to get your project started, find that the code has been passed. Codes are being adopted in some areas over virtually unanimous local opposition. Unlikely? Impossible in democratic America? Listen to what has been happening in my own county in Northern Idaho these past several years.

When I first built underground in 1971 there was no problem; there were no legal restrictions. Then sometime around 1974 or '75 the Federal Government stepped into the picture and began to pressure the county

Hold in your mind the memory of the land,

100

commissioners to adopt the Uniform Building Code. There was even greater pressure, however, on the commissioners to resist. Farmers and ranchers were afraid that they would not be able to build pole barns. Homesteaders were afraid that the codes would be used to harass them. Loggers and retired military personnel didn't like their freedoms messed with. Senior citizens knew that it would jack the price of a home up to the point where they could not build. Virtually everyone in the county bitterly resented eastern suburbanites, who have little concept of real life, dictating to them how they should live. People in a few areas in America are still fiercely independent. The people of Boundary County are among these.

So the commissioners said "no" they would not adopt the Uniform Building Code.

Then the federal authorities began a devious campaign of harassment and intimidation worthy of a bunch of narcotics agents. As reported in the county newspaper, the feds told the commissioners that if they didn't adopt the codes they would each, as individuals, be open to devastating lawsuits in case of flood.

The feds' reasoning went like this: If the Uniform Building Code was not adopted, the residents of Boundary County would not be eligible for Federal Flood Plain Insurance. If the residents did not have Federal Flood Plain Insurance and their homes were wiped out by flood, then the commissioners were at fault and could be sued for everything they had then, and would ever have.

Never noted for great cerebral activity, the commissioners were aghast. That people shouldn't build in flood plains seemed beside the point. That there were private insurance companies did not console them. That the federal authorities themselves were the *real* ones who were stopping the insurance, since they could insure any home they wished with the scratching of a pen, did not occur to them. The commissioners walked around with worried frowns on their faces. They lost sleep at night. Simple folk—store keepers, farmers, retired policemen—they were intimidated. If the feds said that they would lose everything that they had, then it was probably so. The feds were, after all, the biggest guys on the block.

The threat was simple, cunning and terrifying. It was not, however, completely effective. The commissioners feared one thing still more. They feared losing the next election. There may have been even an element of bravery, or defiance, though to suggest this possibility aloud in our county would be to elicit considerable behind-the-hand sniggering. At any rate, to their credit, the commissioners continued to resist.

So the federal government moved the campaign down state. They took it to the state capitol. I'm not sure what pressure tactics the bureaucrats and administrators used—probably part of it was the threat to cut off all federal funds, a favorite form of federal intimidation which is particularly vicious since they blackmail the people with their own money, forcibly collected—but somehow after months of arm twisting they coerced the state legislators into accepting the Uniform Building Code, no doubt to the great relief of county commissioners all over the state who now felt that the pressure was off. This was doubtless part of the federal strategy.

There was immediate uproar. Farmers screamed because they could no longer build pole barns. Homesteaders, loggers, retired military personnel, senior citizens . . . everyone was yelling. The individual state legislators were in danger of losing the next election. So they interpreted the law to apply only to parcels of land under five acres. Everything over five acres was considered to be a farm and as such was declared to be exempt from the building codes. This calmed the uproar somewhat since most Idahoans have land. The others are city people who sit in front of television sets at every conceivable moment shoveling potato chips into their mouths agape. People of this latter group are already intimidated, burned out. Their highest form of political commitment is to pick their noses during the evening news. If the federal government ordered them to stand on their heads two hours per day you would see long lines of them, feet waving in the air.

So there the law lay for six months or a year. Then someone—the state's attorney, I think it was—responding to who knows what pressure, decided that this interpretation of the law was illegal. Farms too, he ruled, would have to come under the

as it is
when
you take it,

101

building codes.

New uproar. Petitions. Angry citizens groups. The state legislators decided then to make the code optional by county decree throwing the burden back upon the commissioners of the individual counties. In our county within the last six months it has been uneasily decided to adopt the codes within the city limits of the county seat, but not in the rural areas. People on farms are temporarily free to build as they wish. For a while. Until the next round of arm twisting.

So you are not safe no matter where you move. Big Brother is going to follow you. Possibly you might get your house down in time, possibly not. Barring some miraculous enlightenment on the part of the majority of Americans, and an unlikely breaking of the corporate/governmental power grip on the lives of the individual citizens, the chances of outrunning the codes are going to get dimmer with each passing month. Consult the *I Ching* on this one. Or ask the Great Potato. If the advice is to move, move fast.

BUILD UNDERGROUND WITH CONCRETE OR OTHER SOCIALLY APPROVED MATERIAL AND BRING THE HOUSE UP TO CODE

This alternative defeats much of the purpose of this book. You don't *want* to build with concrete if you can possibly help it, for all of the reasons stated earlier. And if you try to bring the house up to code it is going to be nearly impossible to survive in the country unless you happen to be independently wealthy.

Every back-to-the-lander is in a bind. If a guy stays on the land and gardens, builds, cuts firewood and the like he has no money for hardware and the other essentials. If he works out—that is, off his land—then he has no time to garden, build, cut firewood. Most homesteaders cope with this by putting in 16 and 18 hour days and by doing it for years, alternating from short term jobs to working on the land. Somehow many of them manage to make it. But building to code is so expensive it virtually wipes out the homesteader's lifestyle. If a guy builds to code he always has to work out. Which is what some people believe is behind the current push for rural codes. The independent, self-reliant Ameri-

can is viewed as a threat in corporate circles. That kind of guy doesn't buy new cars, doesn't buy plasterboard and TV dinners.

Even so, even if you must build with concrete and meet codes, you are still much better off going underground. One Illinois franchiser of concrete underground home construction companies claims that it is possible to build underground and meet all of the codes for as little as half the cost of comparable surface housing.

TRY TO GET A CODE VARIANCE FOR YOUR HOUSE

Variances are *individual* exceptions to the code.

To get a code variance for your project you must first of all be in an area which is served by a variance board. Usually these boards consist of members of the building professions—contractors, building supply people, and the like—all of whom have a vested interest in maintaining the status quo. In other words they are not likely to take a cheerful view of any system which cuts the cost of building from 70% to 90%.

Being desperate you may elect to try this route anyway. One possible ploy which might help is to get a tie-in with a university or governmental funding agency. Underground housing is still experimental and grants are sometimes available. This would give your project the aura of respectability and official approval you so badly need. The concept is not as impossible as it sounds. The Office for Appropriate Technology, Butte, Montana has been pelting me recently with application forms for a federal grant, and they might pelt you too if you drop them a line.

GETTING AN UNDERGROUND HOUSE AMENDMENT TO THE CODES

Amendments are blanket changes in the codes. Unlike variances they apply to everyone in the same situation, not just to individual structures. If you can swing this one you can do your community a real service.

Amendments are legislated by *elected officials*. If your state has codes which are optional by the counties or individual communities you stand a reasonable chance here, for it is the local officials whom you would be dealing with rather than the state legislature. Presumably few if any of them would be in the building trades and thus would not have those vested interests to influence their decisions. Unlike the variance boards, whose members are appointed, the elected officials are susceptible to citizen pressure.

Petitions, gathering groups of like-minded fellow citizens to make your presentation with you, stirring up local interest through publicity—all of these can help here. It also helps considerably if you can persuade an architecture professor from the local college to put in a word. United Stand in California was helped greatly by Sim Van Der Ryn, a U.C. Berkeley professor of architecture. Though you are unlikely to find a man of his caliber, you may still find an aware professor who senses the trend. There often seems to be one such professor in each architecture department.

It is important to emphasize in your presentation that what you are proposing is good for the community, good for the nation. It is good for the community because your home will not be an eyesore. But don't put it that way. All of the elective officials live in eyesores and may take offense. Instead emphasize the beauty of underground architecture, how instead of a surface building you will create a surface garden, a park almost; how it provides small wildlife habitat to the delight and education of children. Point out that whatever noise you create will be muffled before it reaches your neighbors. Explain how vegetation purifies the air and moderates climate. Explain that, rather than a detriment to the neighborhood, underground housing becomes an asset. The "Ecology House" on Cape Cod in Massachusetts, an early, rather bland example of underground architecture, is such an attraction that a fee is charged to visitors.

Underground housing is good for the nation because it conserves building materials and, especially, energy. On October 12, 1976, the *Chicago Daily News* reported, "The government also has entertained thoughts of subterranean dwellings. The Bureau of Standards recently completed a study showing that the nation could save $100 billion in heating costs by 1980 if everyone lived underground." 100 billion. That alone could wipe out America's balance of payments deficit by wiping out our foreign oil imports.

Three books which can help you present a scholarly, erudite presentation are: *Alternatives in Energy Conservation: The Use of Earth Covered Buildings*, printed and distributed by the U.S. Printing Office, and which was prepared for the National Science Foundation Research Applications Directorate; *Earth Integrated Architecture*, published by the Arizona State University College of Architecture Foundation; and *Underground Designs* by architect Malcolm B. Wells.

For other information on how to deal with the codes (though not specifically in regard to underground housing) you should read *The Owner-Builder and The Code, Politics of Building Your Home* by Ken Kern, Ted Kogon and Rob Thallon. Information on ordering these four books is given in the back of this book.

Invaluable advice, sympathy, and the inspiration of learning from a group of owner-builders who successfully challenged the codes may be obtained by contacting United Stand, P.O. Box 191, Potter Valley, Ca. 95469. These folks act as a clearinghouse for communication on code reform. They are supported by the general public and, as such, welcome donations.

CODE EVASION

For those who do not have the time, energy or finances to move, fight for an amendment or comply with the code there is only one alternative left: evasion. The rule of thumb here is go ahead and build first and worry about the legal ramifications later. Except in a few mad instances, the authorities do not raze homes once they have been built.

It is important at the onset to realize that the public utilities usually work with the building department the way the post office works with the FBI to illegally open and read people's mail, the way the telephone company works with the FBI to illegally tap people's phones, the way International Telephone and Telegraph works to illegally overthrow foreign governments (Chile) by cooperating with, and privately financing, the CIA. Corporate America and bureaucratic America have teamed up.

with all your might,

In many cases utility companies will not hook up a house unless they see a portfolio of permits and certificates. They don't stop at just demanding a certificate of wiring inspection by a qualified electrician, but in many cases will demand that the foundation be approved, the plumbing . . . So you are evading the utility companies also.

For middle class families moving to the country to escape the cities, code evasion may seem distasteful. The very idea may be shocking. For long-haired back-to-the-landers it is a means of circumventing yet another set of laws, many of which were specifically written to harass those not in the mainstream of American life.

Evasive tactics fall into two broad categories: partial compliance, and total evasion.

Partial compliance is resorted to when the home is to be built in an area which is visible from roads or to neighbors, and when that home is to be serviced by the public utilities. Such homes as these tend to come to the attention of building inspectors.

One common tactic to get around the inspectors and the utilities by partial compliance is to build a central, or core, unit first which meets the minimum requirements of the code. In the case of the Uniform Building Code (one of the four national codes and the one most commonly adopted by the western states) this means constructing a house which has at least 150 square feet of free floor space in one room. When this central unit has passed the various inspections and has been serviced by the utilities, the owner constructs "farm buildings"—which are in some places code exempt—and which are nearby or adjoining the original unit. The "farm buildings" are quietly wired with a line from the central unit and are covertly modified for human use. In the case of underground housing it may mean building the central unit of concrete and the "underground farm buildings" by the PSP system. Be sure to build enough doorways in the concrete to facilitate the joining of the units later on.

A variation is to build a barn, tool shed, chicken coop or similar structure, get it hooked up legally and then extend the line to an outlaw building. These structures can also provide a "front," a reason for the sound of hammers and saws which may deceive possi-bly hostile neighbors while you work on your illegal building.

One lady in Northern Idaho, upon being denied a hook-up, gently told a power company executive, "All right, I guess I'll have to set up a wind generator." Two days later a crew was out to hook up her house without comment—and without asking to see any certificates of inspection.

In one of his books, Ken Kern offers a tactic to deal with inspectors and building departments. Since these bureaucrats are sometimes officious, and occasionally seem bent upon harassing owner-builders by "throwing the book at them," Kern suggests that you throw the book right back. You can do this by continually demanding inspections of the smallest details. When they begin to balk at coming out twice a day, harass them with seemingly sincere phone calls every hour to ask such things as what nail size you should use for the framing 2x4's, how many glazier's points must go around each window, what are the specifications of glazier's putty, how thick must it be, and so on. A couple from Michigan recently reported that several weeks of this finally drove the local building inspector to yell, "Stop it! Stop it! Just go ahead and *build* your house!" He hasn't been seen or heard from since.

Total evasion of the codes may be achieved by hiding your house altogether. Though areas so remote as to make this ploy practical are becoming hard to find, it is still possible and frequently done.

Houses are sometimes hidden deep in the woods, over high ridges or across deep ravines. Though it is tough to get the materials in, it's also tough for the building inspector to get in. In time your woods will become as familiar and friendly to you as a thicket is to a rabbit. To a building inspector, however, the woods will seem hostile and unfriendly. He's out of his element once he has to get off the pavement and out of his car, or away from that desk full of papers and citations he so lovingly shuffles about for hours on end. He'll be *totally* lost if he can't find a trail. Trails can be disguised by a number of methods.

Helicopter surveillance is becoming so common the 'copters outnumber the hummingbirds these days. Though it is most commonly the sheriff up looking for those "outlaw gardens" sometimes these departments swap information. (Many young midwestern farmers were busted when the Department of Agriculture aerial photo planes, up taking pictures to see that the farmers were not exceeding crop acreage allotments, spotted a patch of "different vegetation" where the farmer thought it was safely hidden in the middle of hundreds of acres of corn. The USDA routinely turns such photos over to the Department of Justice.)

Underground housing is a means of defeating even the aerial snoops. If you are willing to dig your house deep in the woods thereby foregoing the considerable benefits of an attached sunken greenhouse you may build a house which is virtually undetectable from the air. They might spot bright lights at night through the trees so watch that angle. (Game wardens are the "bears in the air" at night, up looking for poachers "spotlighting" deer.) The only other way they could spot your house is by the wood smoke. Burning dry wood with the stove vents opened properly should eliminate most of the hazard there. So will a good wind. In an emergency the stove pipe may be lifted off and the stove capped with a pie tin so the home doesn't become smoked up. The Viet Cong hid *whole armies* in the woods underground, defeating the best efforts of hundreds of thousands of men armed with the most sophisticated detection devices, equipment that the local authorities will have neither time nor budget to employ.

About your greenhouse: In this case build it out in the open, sunken into a southern slope. This will distract and mislead the airborne snoops. It could also provide you hours of merriment when, thinking that they've finally located your home, the authorities discover that they are busting a greenhouse full of tomatoes.

Remember that renovations and additions are supposed to fall under the code. Any sudden building spree at a site which is visible may incur the wrath of the authorities. You have an advantage here in building underground since it is hard to see just what you are doing. A tall fence built around your project will make it virtually undetectable

from ground level. In the case of possible spotter aircraft a few beams thrown across the excavation and some black polyethylene drug across that should give you hasty camouflage, yet another advantage unique to underground housing. Imagine trying to camouflage even a one story above-ground house. Keep the polyethylene over the project when no work is being done.

The authorities cannot issue citations if they do not know what is going on. Since they cannot afford the time to go around checking every home they sometimes use other people. Some utility companies have turned their meter readers into informers looking for unauthorized renovations and additions. They don't seem to be using children yet, that ploy having gotten a dirty name when used by other countries, but at least one community has reportedly made informers out of the garbage men.

preserve it for your children,

In the study, the author composes an abusive letter to his senator.

and love it as God loves us all.

Sad to say, the greatest amount of informing is done by unfriendly neighbors. When moving to a new rural area you may be received with hostility, though this may not be apparent at the time. You may notice a certain coolness, a tight-lipped reserve. There are many reasons for this reaction ranging from fear that you may influence their children in a negative way (dope, sex), to the fear that you will make a lot of noise or build something gross or litter your land with junk. People live in the country because they like it, and your presence there makes it that much less country. They may have used your property for years in the friendly way country people have of sharing land. They may have traditionally hunted on it, or picked berries there, or picnicked. It might have been owned by their family at one time. Your presence there may deny them these uses of the land, deny them their heritage. They dread and resent beyond words the "No Trespassing" signs so many new people put up. Country people are conservative, slow to change. They resent any abrupt change in their neighborhood whether it be physical or social. Newcomers represent these changes and thus sometimes seem a threat. If they have come from a city their lifestyles are almost certain to be different. There is an unwritten country more which says that you may do pretty near anything you wish as long as you don't show it. Unfortunately newcomers—especially young ones—often consider this hypocrisy and seem to go out of their way to flaunt the differences.

Strange to say, you too may resent it in a few years when some clown comes crowding in on the land next to yours.

So it's to your advantage as well as for their peace of mind to keep a low profile when moving into the country. Don't make waves, at least until they get to know and accept you. Not only might this courtesy keep them from calling the building inspector and other authorities down on you but it has its positive side. It can open doors and turn you on to sources of information. Country people, especially the older ones (the most conservative), are walking encyclopedias of how-to-do-it information. They love to talk. They will be reticent at first about offering information or criticism since they don't wish to interfere in your life, but once they see that you are eager for knowledge they will begin an endless stream of anecdotes and tips. Slowly too you will come to the realization that they are just as big outlaws as you are. Many of them poach and some of them have been making whiskey for a half century. They can no more go into town to get a permit to rebuild their chicken coop than can you. Country life would cease if that were the case. They can be mighty good friends if you give them half a chance.

RULE~OF~THUMB ENGINEERING TABLES

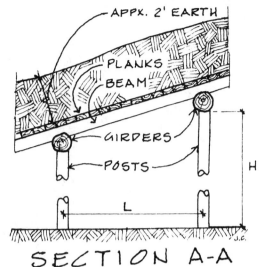

These tables are meant to be guides only, not the final word on your engineering problems. Consult them when designing and making posts, girders and beams so that you may work up material of sufficient girth. You are supposed to get competent individual engineering advice before building.

A structure built to these specifications will support the load of two feet of earth plus the equivalent of one foot of water (how much snow that equals depends upon how wet the snow is.) There is a certain amount of error computed into the tables so don't give up your project if your dimensions or materials don't exactly match what we have here.

SECTION A-A

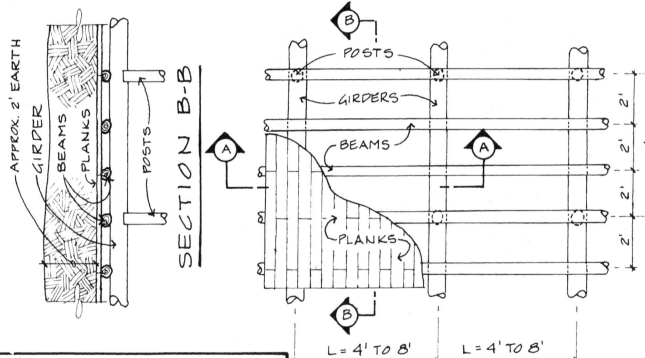

SECTION B-B

L = 4' TO 8'   L = 4' TO 8'

TABLE 1					
LENGTH	BEAM		GIRDER		POST
L (FEET)	ROUND (DIA.)	RECT. (NOM.*)	ROUND (DIA.)	RECT. (NOM.*)	H=APPX. 10' (DIAMETER)
(a) 4'	5"	3×6 (2×8)	8"	4×10	5"
(b) 5'	6"	4×6 (2×10)	8½"	6×8 (3×12)	6"
(c) 6'	7"	4×8	9"	6×10 (4×12)	6"
(d) 7'	7"	6×8 (3×10)	9½"	6×10 (4×12)	7"
(e) 8'	7½"		10"		7"

MATERIAL:
PLANKS: PONDEROSA OR FIR/LARCH
BEAMS & GIRDERS: FIR/LARCH
POSTS: CEDAR OR LODGEPOLE PINE

LAYOUT:
3/4" PLANKS; 2' SPACING OF BEAMS;
4' TO 8' SPACING OF GIRDERS;
8' SPACING OF POSTS.

A. TIVERIOS, ENGINEER

Our initial consideration when setting up these tables was the thickness of the boards or planks which went on the roof and the distance they could span. It was decided that 2' was about as long as you should go between beams with the 3/4'' boards, and that 1½'' boards could reasonably span 3'6''. There will be a two foot spacing then from center to center of the beams for the first two tables (which deal with 3/4'' material) and a three and one half foot spacing between the beams for Tables 3 and 4.

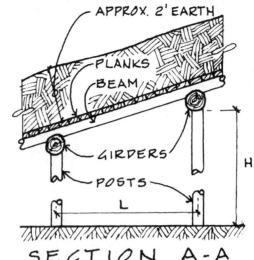

SECTION A-A

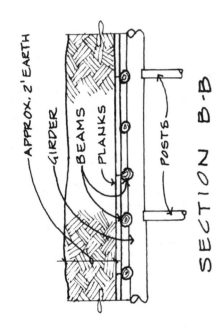

SECTION B-B

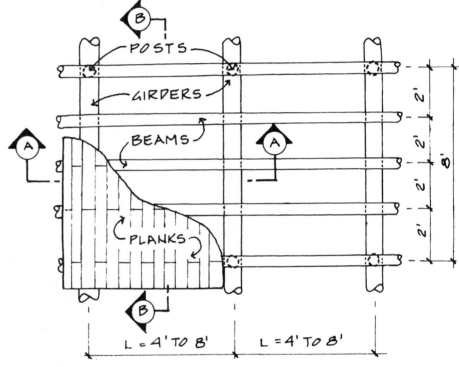

PLAN

LAYOUT:
3/4'' PLANKS;
2' SPACING OF BEAMS;
4' TO 8' GIRDER SPACING;
8' SPACING OF POSTS.

MATERIAL:
SAME.

TABLE 2					
LENGTH	BEAM		GIRDER		POST
L	ROUND	RECT.	ROUND	RECT.	H=APPX. 10'
(FEET)	(DIA.)	(NOM.)	(DIA.)	(NOM.)	(DIAMETER)
(a) 4'	5''	3×6 (2×8)	9½''	3×16	5''
(b) 5'	6''	4×6 (2×10)	10½''	4×16	7''
(c) 6'	7''	4×8	11''	4×16	7''
(d) 7'	7''	6×8 (3×10)	12''	6×14	8''
(e) 8'	7½''		12½''	—	8''

108

Our next consideration was the distance between the posts. We tackled this by setting up each table according to how far the posts are spaced which support each individual girder. On Table 1 the posts beneath each girder are 6' apart. On Table 2 they are 8' apart. On Table 3 they are 7' and for Table 4 they are 10'6" apart.

There is a second spacing of posts, however, determined by how far apart the girders are placed. This is indicated on each chart by the letter "L" (for length of span of the beams between girders). Each table gives you a choice of span in this direction of from 4' to 8'.

An example: Let's say we are about to build the Shed Roof Flat Land Design which has all posts equally 6' apart. We would go to Table 1 (6' spacing of posts under the girders) and consult line (c) which has an "L" (distance between girders) of 6'.

Reading across the line then, we see that with 3/4" roof planking and 6' x 6' spacing of posts we need beams with a minimum diameter of 7", girders which have a diameter of 9" and posts which are at least 6" in diameter.

Here's another example: Let's say we are building a 14' x 16' room (or house) and want as few posts in the center as possible. There are two ways of approaching this depending upon which way we run our girders.

If the girders are to span the 14' width we would need three of them—two along the walls and one up through the center of the room. We would space our posts 7 feet apart under the girders which would send us to Table 3. Since our girders themselves would be 8' apart we would consult under line (e) to find that our beams would have to be 9½", our girders 11½" in diameter and our posts 8". The planking would, of course, be 1½".

If the girders are to run the 16' length we would support them with posts 8' apart sending us to Table 2. The girders in this case would be 7' apart so we would consult line (d) where we find we need beams 7", girders 12" and posts 8" in diameter. The planking in this case would be 3/4".

*THAT IS, NOMINAL DIMENSIONS, WHICH YOU ASK FOR AT THE LUMBER STORE. ACTUAL DIMENSIONS SLIGHTLY SMALLER. TABLES ALLOW FOR THIS.

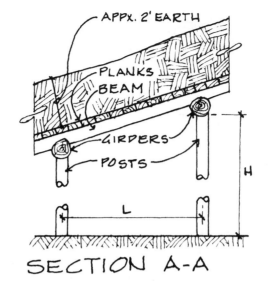

SECTION A-A

LAYOUT:
1½" THICK PLANKS.
3'-6" BEAM SPACING.
4' TO 8' GIRDER SPACING.
7' POST SPACING.

MATERIAL:
SAME.

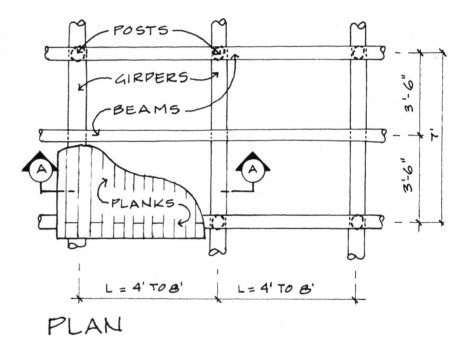

PLAN

TABLE 3						
	LENGTH	BEAM		GIRDER		POST
	L (FEET)	ROUND (DIA.)	RECT. (NOM.)*	ROUND (DIA.)	RECT. (NOM.)*	H=APPX. 10' (DIAMETER)
(a)	4'	6"	3×8 (2×10)	9"	6×10	5"
(b)	5'	7"	3×10	9½"	3×16	6"
(c)	6'	8"	4×10	10½"	4×14	7"
(d)	7'	8½"	6×10	11"	4×16	7"
(e)	8'	9½"	6×10	11½"	4×16	8"

109

The tables are computed for ponderosa pine planking, fir or larch girders and beams and for lodgepole pine or cedar posts. A certain amount of substitution of material may be made. Almost any pine may be substituted for ponderosa, for example.

Here are comparisons of bending strengths of a few species of lumber:

If Ponderosa pine has a strength of 1.00
Douglas fir has 1.17
Cedar .... .83
Aspen .... .78
Lodgepole pine .... .92

A final word here: we recommend using posts which are a good deal thicker than the minimum listed in the tables. This is for several reasons. The first is a psychological or aesthetic reason; at a glance the posts will seem too thin. If you are making the largest span listed in the tables, the 8' x 10'6" listed under e of Table 4, you will see that 9" posts are expected to support 9½" beams and 14" girders. While you and I and the engineers realize that a 9" post will do this since the post is primarily employed for compressive strength rather than for shear strength, it may well seem alarming to visitors or even to yr. mate. A good thick post will seem more reassuring.

A second reason for using thick posts is that they will rot through much more slowly where buried.

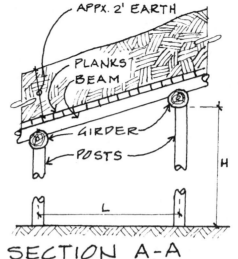

SECTION A-A

LAYOUT:
1½" THICK PLANKS.
3'·6" BEAM SPACING.
4' TO 8' GIRDER SPACING.
10'·6" POST SPACING.

MATERIAL: SAME.

PLAN

L = 4' TO 8'   L = 4' TO 8'

TABLE 4					
LENGTH L (FEET)	BEAM		GIRDER*		POST
	ROUND (DIA.)	RECT. (NOM.)	ROUND (DIA.)	RECT. (NOM.)	H=APPX. 10' (DIAMETER)
(a) 4'	6"	2×10	11½" (2·9")	4×16	7"
(b) 5'	7"	3×10	12" (2·9½")	2·3×16	7"
(c) 6'	8"	4×10	13" (2·10")	2·4×14	8"
(d) 7'	8½"	6×10	13½" (2·10½")	2·6×12	9"
(e) 8'	9½"	6×10	14" (2·11½")	—	9"

*HERE TWO GIRDERS MAY BE USED TO REPLACE SINGLE GIRDER. THIS ALLOWS GIRDERS TO BE SMALLER, MORE MANAGEABLE, AND MORE EASILY OBTAINABLE.

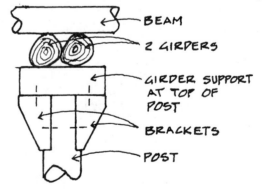

DRAWING ABOVE SHOWS ONE METHOD OF SUPPORTING 2 GIRDERS WITH SINGLE POST. NOTE: WOOD IS ACCEPTABLE MATERIAL FOR BRACKETS AND GIRDER SUPPORT.

110

New Approved Design Methods

Study this page carefully. It contains six new Approved Methods of Design which will give you views and light while draining the water off the structure downhill onto solid earth. (A seventh is an extended Hollywood wing, not pictured.) These new methods are explained fully in **The Low-Cost Underground House Workshop video set**. See last page.

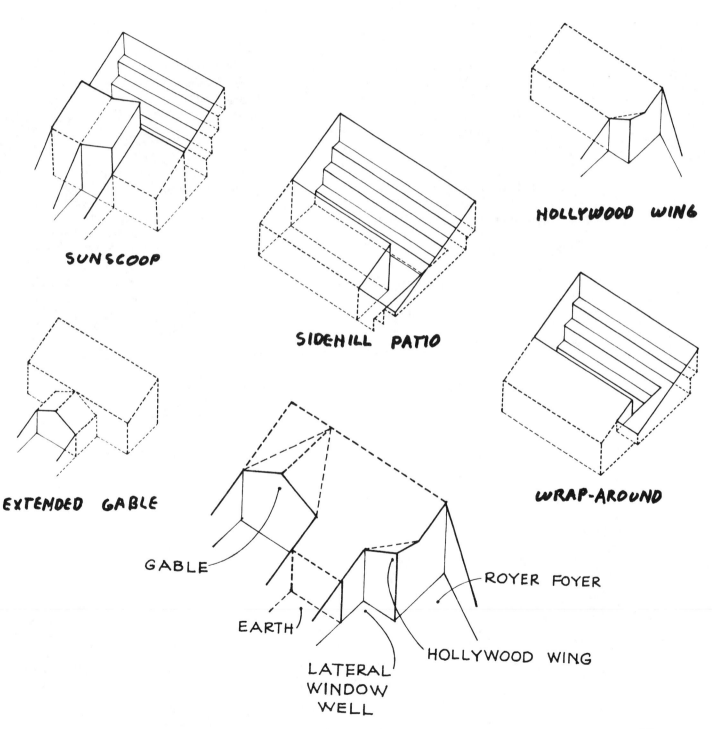

SUNSCOOP

SIDEHILL PATIO

HOLLYWOOD WING

EXTENDED GABLE

WRAP-AROUND

GABLE

EARTH

LATERAL WINDOW WELL

HOLLYWOOD WING

ROYER FOYER

Even the whiteman cannot be exempt from the common destiny.

The preceding letter to the President of the United States was written by Chief Seathl of the Duwamish tribe, State of Washington, in 1855, regarding the proposed purchase of the tribe's land.

About Mole Publishing & Contributors

This is the first book ever produced by Mole Publishing Company. Mole is an acronym for Mike Oehler's Literary Enterprises (cute, eh?). Oehler, the alert reader will recall, is the author. This is a self-published book.

Why publish your own? Well, why build your own house, or grow your own vegetables or raise your own meat? Why make love when you can watch a porno film? Can you imagine what the New York Literary Establishment would have done to this book? They would have sterilized it, deodorized it, pasteurized it, homogenized it, added herbicides, fungicides, pesticides, preservatives and emulsifiers, artificial color and flavoring. They would have put a naked lady on the cover and changed the title to *Cave House of Passion*. No thanks.

About the Engineer

The man who devised the engineering tables was Antonio Tiverios, a registered structural engineer who built most of his own home, and who has had many years of professional underground construction experience. He is currently engineering an expansion to the Chicago subway system.

Many people contributed to the making of this book. Among them are Jo Dee Simard, typing; Ellen Frank, Sarah Royer and Beatrice McGuire, proofreading; Lynn Moore, photograph page 16; Edgar Stephenson, photographs on pages 17, 20, 21, 22; John Clark, lettering and art work; Lester Dore, pasteup and calligraphy of Chief Seathl's letter; Dave Scott, layout suggestions; Gary Kokes, cover help.

The type was set by The Typesetters, Camilla, Glenn and Kurt, Kenilworth, Ill. The color page was printed by Triangle Printers, Skokie, Ill. The bulk of the book was printed in Chelsea, Michigan by Book-Crafters, Inc.

About the Illustrator

The illustrator was Christopher Royer, who has studied at Earlham College, Boston Architectural Center, and is finishing up his degree in Architecture and Planning at the University of Massachusetts. He has worked as a staff member at the NACUL Environmental Design Center, Amherst, and has been involved in a variety of construction jobs on both conventional and experimental structures. He and his wife, Sarah, live in Northampton, Mass.

112

Update

We write this update for the sixth printing nineteen years after publishing the first edition. How — the reader will want to know — have the designs and theories withstood the test of time? Have we made any new discoveries or changes?

The designs and theories have stood up well — beautifully, in fact. Someone wrote recently from Washington state to say he had heard a rumor that we had renounced the PSP system and the Five Methods of design. He didn't believe the rumor but wanted to check it out before beginning to build from the book. We told him to build with confidence. Rumors of that sort are started by failed architects — concrete terrorists to a man — doddering, red-eyed, Skid Row inhabitants who clutch pints of Mad Dog between trembling hands. Give them a quarter if they approach, but pay them no mind.

As to whether we have made any new discoveries or changes, the answer is yes and yes. We now have seven more approved methods of design, five of which will help you get those coveted downhill views. On page 111 of this sixth edition we have included drawings of six of the new methods (the seventh is an extended Hollywood wing.) Study that page carefully before designing if you do not have The Low Cost Underground House Workshop Video Set (see last page). Note that in all cases the drainage has been taken care of—water on the roof runs off onto solid earth on the downhill side. Not so easily detected is that the lateral window well extends windows from the gable to the Hollywood wing in an unbroken line allowing someone standing inside an oblique view downhill.

The reader/viewer/designers who do best are those who study the material again and again and who follow the design methods to the letter. Those who do worst think they are being creative by coming up with a "new" design because they think it is different from anything in this book. Ah, the poor, dumb people. With one solitary exception the "new" designs these misguided souls have told me abut have been some variation of the First Thought house, and frequently these designs have led to disaster. Just off the top of my head I can name you three houses which are in trouble or worse, because they were not built according to the approved methods. On one house the roof earth kept washing off and splattering those downhill windows with mud. The owner's palliative to this dilemma was to shore up the downhill section of the roof and install drain tile to try to run the water off to the side. In the end what this did was to back the water up behind the overhang and over the top of the gently sloping roof where it searched out flaws in the polyethylene and leaked.

The second First Thought disaster caused the owner/builder so much drainage trouble that he is pulling the roof off and re-designing it altogether. And the third? That unfortunate guy approached me at a barter fair and shook my hand and said, "If we had had your book before we built we could have saved ourselves years of work. We built a First Thought house and it has given us so much drainage trouble that we are abandoning it altogether. We're building from your book this time."

Sad stories, but true.

Is the First Thought house always a disaster? No, but you are running a heavy chance of severe trouble in the years ahead. You *must* design so that it is easier for water to run off *away* from the house than to back up against a wall — whether it is concrete or PSP. If it backs up you make gravity your implacable enemy for the life of that house. Solve your drainage problems *first*. Run that water off *down* the hill. Then work hard for those downhill views with the approved methods of design.

We throw out a rule-of-thumb here: make sure that at least one half of the downhill side of the house is solid earth. "But," you may wail, "I want that sweeping view. I want to catch as much sunlight as possible for passive solar energy. I want a greenhouse on that south side."

Okay, assuming that you are able to site that First Thought house on a south slope, look at what happens: You build a place with all of your windows facing south giving you a sweeping view down your valley or ravine. But now you decide you want a greenhouse. You believe that the most energy-efficient way of attaching the greenhouse is to those south windows, so you do that. Presto, you have a greenhouse. But now you have also lost a good deal of the direct solar gain in the interior of your house which you had through those south windows; the plants and new wall intercept much of the sunlight. They also block much of your sweeping view.

Remember that by putting in the Uphill Patio you get that greenhouse and free those downhill windows for view and direct solar gain. The windows on the uphill side become an indirect source of solar gain since the temperature in the greenhouse on most sunny days will be higher than that of the house. Then, too, you may bounce some sunlight down into the house with mirrors. (On a north slope the Uphill Patio windows admit *direct* sunlight most of the day.) Or you may blow that heat into the house with a small fan. And you get that cross ventilation, balance of light, escape route, drainage benefit, etc., etc.

Perhaps some readers believe that by building from the basic design and following the design methods religiously their creativity may be compromised. Owner/builders are notoriously protective of their design freedom. They often resent even professional help, and I know of at least one alternative architect who gave up his practice because "owner/builders never listen to you."

Using the Basic Design and the approved design methods does not hinder creativity, but enhances it. What we are giving you are the *tools* to design with. If you wished to paint, would your creativity be compromised if we gave you a set of oil paints or watercolors? And so it is with the design methods. The creativity comes in what you *do* with them, for the design possibilities are almost infinite.

As for changes, the single really major one that we have made in the past several years is that WE NO LONGER RECOMMEND THE USE OF PENTA FOR POST TREATMENT. Penta (pentachlorophenol) does not entirely stay fixed in the treated wood. Much of it leaches out to move around in the environment. In 1976 researchers from the chemistry department tested students at Florida State University, Tallahassee, and discovered that, while 36 percent of the dormitory students had measurable levels of 2,3,5-T and Silvex

(herbicides) in their urine, virtually every student tested showed traces of penta.

Pentachlorophenol contains HxCDD, OCDD and hepta-CDD, three dioxins which the Vermont Public Interest Research Group, among others, considers to be of great concern from the standpoint of public health. Penta has reportedly been placed under restriction by the Canadian government. I believe it is off the retail market in the U.S. now also, and may be applied only by licensed professionals. It is definitely recommended that penta not be used within a home, if anywhere.

A rumor has it that in the old days farmers treated their fence posts with creosote from their stovepipes, that they went to the store-bought preservatives only because their farms and fences got too large for the amount of creosote produced at home, and presumably, because many abandoned the wood stove. I suspect they mixed the creosote with diesel fuel or kerosene. Folks at the U.S. Forest Service Forest Products Laboratory in Madison, Wisconsin tell me that stove pipe creosote and commercial creosote made from coal tar are chemically the same. I have considerable reservations about the commercial product since the EPA tends to wring its hands about its toxicity. On the other hand mankind has been in contact with natural creosote presumably since the discovery of fire. Natural creosote is the result of incomplete combustion of wood. Presumably all the steaks that have fallen in campfires through the ages and brushed off and eaten, and all whisky that has been aged in charred oak barrels has picked up natural creosote. I confess I am confused.

So I have developed another system. I now char my posts where they are to go into the ground. It hardens the wood, forms its own creosote and makes a charcoal layer around the wood that most critters do not care to eat. This old farmer's trick gives a post probably at least a 50 percent greater life span when in contact with the earth.

But I do more. Where the post is to be used indoors I wrap the charred end in five polyethylene garbage bags (non-biogradable) and tape them down. Sometimes I cover the bags with a section of newspaper to protect them from rocks in the soil. Then I set the posts making sure that the garbage bags come a couple of inches above floor level. I call this the "barrier method."

There is one other method which is acceptable. It involves using our old friendly enemy, concrete.

You may pour "piers" in holes you have dug on the site with a post hole digger, holes you have reinforced with chicken wire and half-inch rebar. Or you may pre-fab the piers by pouring concrete in greased six or eight inch stove pipe, loosely held closed with plumbers tape. Post and pier are joined by a rebar set in the concrete which fits into a hole in the bottom of the post. Caution: this system may "hinge" – may push in due to the lateral thrust.

Or you may pour footings. These have the advantage of great strength. The posts should neither sink nor "hinge." But footings are labor intensive and expensive. They emit radon gas and could possibly be unstable during an earthquake.

Of all the systems, my favorite is just charring the posts and wrapping them in garbage bags. At least for interior use it is. Reader Doug Brecht in upstate N.Y. wants to know, "What exactly is it that causes your PSP system to fall short of the codes? The fact that the wood is not treated?" Right. We contacted a member of the International Conference of Building Officials — the people who write the Uniform Building Code – for an interpretation. U houses must meet the requirements for all-weather wood basement construction, which means pressure treated wood. (The official was also upset that "these underground houses don't have windows in the bedrooms" and other design violations such as entrances only on one side of the house – all of which can be overcome by following closely the design ideas advanced in this book.) The official, incidentally, was astonished to learn that they have no objection to the earth/carpet floor. The only thing in the code about flooring is that the bathroom and garage both must have hard impermeable surfaces. I hope they are not going to rush out and write something into the code now. ("George! George! People in Idaho are putting carpets down on the earth, calling that a floor and we have nothing in the code to stop them!")

The codes are not insurmountable. William Howat, Sunnyside, Washington, got a variance for the PSP method in Yakima County, Washington. He got written testimonials from prior PSP builders as to the durability of buried polyethylene, and the variance board passed it. A precedent has been set.

Special note by the author: The diagram on page 44 has led many people to think that the roof over the clerestories drains down over the windows. Nothing of the sort. We never place our clerestories so that they interrupt the drainage flow. They do not go across the roof, but up and down it, or at an oblique angle. Please note the illustrations on page 45. If the man on page 44 is sitting in the house on page 45, the roof drains off to his right.

– M.O., April 1997

NEWEST UPDATE

Our progress in underground design and construction is almost entirely by trial and error. We write the books because we pioneer the methods. In most cases only time will tell of our success or failures. The following is an update on what we have learned in recent years.

Wood in a Post/Shoring/Polyethylene underground structure rots at different rates depending upon the design, material and the use of the structure. Three cases illustrate extremes. The first is the root cellar accessed through the secret panel in the flatland house as seen in our videos. The wood in this root cellar rotted out in just a half dozen years. There were two mistakes quickly apparent: the roof of the building adjoining it leaked and drained into the root cellar, and there was inadequate ventilation.

Case two is my PSP underground sauna built around 1977. This lasted beautifully for the 18 years it was a sauna, but after it was disused and became an impromptu root cellar, the wood rotted quickly.

Case three is my $500 underground house. It started as the $50 house in 1971 and grew into the $500 model in 1975. The original house is today's bedroom. Despite occasional roof leaks the wood is holding up beautifully. The difference? One is that there is a vapor barrier, polyethylene, beneath the carpet. Water vapor rises from the bare earth floor in the other two. A second is that there is adequate ventilation what with the frequent opening of doors and windows. A third is the wood stove which heats the home and dries the wood, checking, no doubt, the fungal decay. Remember that the sauna didn't start to rot till the fires went out.

The moral here? Wooden root cellars are problematical. I still think they can be done

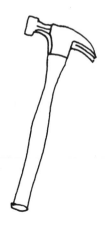

with: (1) A layer of polyethylene buried four to six inches beneath the earthen floor, or under wood planking; (2) Adequate ventilation through one or two six-inch stove pipes or plastic pipes; and (3) the wall and roofing wood either saturated in boiled linseed oil or coated with several coats of polyurethane outdoor varnish or painted. Would I build a root cellar with cinder block? NO! Not unless it was very old salvaged cinder block. Some of today's manufacturers, research tells me, are now putting the incredibly toxic ash from garbage incinerators into cinder block as a way of disposing of a substance no country on earth will accept. Would I build a root cellar with concrete? With funds available, probably. With rock? If I had rock on my land, you bet! That's the traditional way. Since I don't have rock, I'll continue to experiment with PSP root cellars. Check with me twenty years down the line for success. As for PSP family shelters, I'd advise all the above (polyethylene under the floor, linseed oil, varnish or paint) plus attaching them to the house and using them for other daily things to keep the air flowing, or, in stand-alone models, to fire up the heater periodically to dry out the fungi.

Will I continue to build my homes with PSP? Absolutely! I'm in the process of building the Ridge House this way. One notable probable improvement, however: I will add a layer of EPDM synthetic rubber swimming pool and pond liner for roof waterproofing. Might even try some on the walls. I'm not hung up on polyethylene. The point is to keep water off the wood and any substance which will do this should probably be investigated. EPDM seems to be the most promising improvement so far. Building inspectors should like this too.

–M.O., November 2004

IMPORTANT NOTE

Having read about, designed, consulted, built or visited some hundreds of underground houses over the past thirty five years, Mike Oehler has concluded that the single most important element in the success and livability of an underground home is the design. And it is clear to him that most people going underground are failing miserably in this area. This includes, unfortunately, the great majority of professional architects.

To answer this need Mike has created "The Low-cost Underground House Workshop and Shelter Seminar," a three-tape, six-hour video set. It shows places built with the PSP system including several on his own land. It teaches how to build a low-cost shelter which will take families through nearly anything, and how to build a wonderfully effective earth-sheltered greenhouse. But what makes the set truly unique is the design course in the second tape.

The design course takes approximately four hours additional time to complete. It is the same material, using the same scale models that Mike has taught for over thirty years in Canada, England, Scotland, Belgium, Germany, the Netherlands and twenty-six American States, often sponsored by university architectural departments.

In the course the viewer becomes a participant by actually designing five underground houses – ones on north, south, east and west slopes, and one on flat land – using the copyrighted workbook and design kit which is provided free. You learn to design so that you get windows from all four directions of the compass in each and every room in each and every house. That's too many windows of course, but it gives you the ability to design windows from at least two directions for cross ventilation, a balance of light and actual sunlight into every underground room. All that and good views too.

Having abundant light, air and views in an underground house adds tens of thousands of dollars to the resale value over the normal dark underground house with its scant windows, not to mention your own pleasure and pride in the home. Mike now has thirteen approved methods of design instead of just the five mentioned in this book. Only the videos can do them justice.